D1524569

Winnetka-Northfield Public Library

3 1240 00725 1569

DECEMBER 2023

Withdrawn

Winnetka-Northfield Public
Library District
Winnetka, IL 60093
(847) 446-7220

THE GOOD LUCK BOOK

A Celebration of Global Traditions, Superstitions, and Folklore

WRITTEN BY

Heather Alexander

ILLUSTRATED BY

Ruth Burrows, Teo Georgiev, Sonny Ross, and Sarah Walsh

Contents

AUTHOR'S NOTE

I decided to write this book because I was curious about so many of my quirky superstitions and good luck charms.

How did they come to be? Is there any logic behind them? As I researched, and friends and family near and far shared their own beliefs, I was surprised how many we all had in common. I've tried to include as many superstitions as possible here, but, honestly, I could've filled several more books, and I apologize if I've left out your favorite! For a lot of the entries, I had to choose just one country where a certain superstition is popular. If you find yourself saying, "We do that too!" it's because several places often have some version of the same superstition, but often with small differences. One of the trickier jobs was determining if something is a superstition, cultural tradition, or religion. Often the line is blurred, and what one person sees as a superstition, another sees as a belief. Finding the origin and explanation for many superstitions and beliefs was a challenge, because, over the years, some have gotten mixed up, combined with others, or the original meaning has been lost. I definitely learned a *lot* of interesting stuff, and I hope you'll have as much fun reading this book as I had writing it (with my lucky pen, of course!), and may fortune always smile upon you!

Introduction

ARE YOU SUPERSTITIOUS?

Have you ever wished on an eyelash? Said "rabbit rabbit" on the first day of the month? Worn your lucky sweatpants to cheer on your favorite team? Or thrown your furniture out of the window?

These are all superstitions, and most people—whether they admit it or not—are a little superstitious every now and then. Humans do all sorts of things based on superstitions, even though we know it may not be very logical or scientific. Often, we don't even realize some of our actions—like covering our mouths when we yawn—are actually derived from superstitions.

WHAT ARE SUPERSTITIONS?

Let's start with a definition. A superstition is an irrational belief, or a belief not based in knowledge or fact. Superstitious thinking often starts out something like this: If I pick my nose, then I'll get a perfect grade on my math quiz. Makes no sense, does it?

But what if one time you happened to pick your nose before a quiz, and you got a perfect grade. And then before the next quiz, you think, "Hmmmmm... why not?" So you pick your nose again and—whoa!—you ace the test again. Now your brain has linked two random things that logically don't have anything to do with one another, but you conclude that picking your nose gives you luck in school. You've somehow forgotten that you paid attention in class, did all the homework problems, and studied (a lot!). Instead, your brain got stuck on an action or object that you falsely believe made something good happen, so you repeat it. Again and again. You tell your friends, and they start picking their noses before quizzes too. And then you all grow up and tell your kids to do it! That's how a superstition is born.

ARE SUPERSTITIONS NEW?

Superstitions are not new. They date back to the beginning of civilization. When people didn't understand something about nature or themselves—such as a massive thunderstorm or a case of the hiccups—they often relied on their own powers of observation. This method brought about tons of great scientific discoveries. But it also led to some false beliefs when our brains failed to register that some causes and effects didn't actually go together, such as whistling on a boat bringing about a storm or an acorn in your pocket preventing old age. But by giving a clear set of rules to follow—if I do this, then this will (or won't) happen—superstitions were often able to help our ancestors feel safer and make sense of what felt senseless. Superstitions and traditions were passed down by word of mouth from generation to generation. The wisdom was bite-sized and easy-to-remember, which probably helped people to recall and repeat them.

"It's not true, but I believe it."
Old saying from Naples, Italy

ARE SUPERSTITIONS ABOUT GOOD LUCK OR BAD LUCK?

They're about both. Even though we've all heard certain bad luck superstitions and beliefs—such as don't walk under a ladder or break a mirror—there are many more about attracting good luck. That's why we often carry a lucky object or charm or pick up a penny, and why there are so many wonderful ways to make a wish.

DO PEOPLE STILL BELIEVE IN SUPERSTITIONS?

Absolutely! Superstitions still have a hold on us today. Even though we know so much more now, a lot in our world still feels out of our control. Repeating certain behaviors—known as rituals—often makes us feel less anxious and nervous. Athletes and performers tend to have a lot of superstitious rituals. Also, many of our beliefs have been taught to us by our families and communities. They've become woven into our everyday lives, and we often accept superstitious beliefs because everyone around us accepts them.

IS IT OKAY TO BE A LITTLE SUPERSTITIOUS?

Yes! Some people believe wholeheartedly in superstition, while others roll their eyes. But many of us fall somewhere in the middle, and we'll knock on wood "just in case." We all choose what we believe in, and it doesn't have to be the same. The most important thing is to continue to make smart choices and search for real answers instead of relying on false connections.

So let's step carefully, cross our fingers, and explore some superstitions, beliefs, and traditions from around the world!

ANIM

Humans have lived side by side with all kinds of animals for centuries and quickly noticed that they smelled, heard, and saw things we couldn't. Animals sensed danger and seemed to predict the weather long before humans did. Could these curious abilities be connected to something magical or mystical? Now, remember—we're talking about a time when people knew little about an animal's biology or what caused its behavior, so they filled in the gaps with superstition. Creatures that ate a farmer's crops or preyed upon livestock were mistrusted, and people celebrated the animals they found helpful.

Some animal superstitions and beliefs may make you giggle, but many have real consequences for the animals themselves. Animals thought to bring misfortune—as well as those with "lucky" body parts—are often hunted, sometimes to the point of becoming endangered. The animals are counting on us to set our superstitions and traditional beliefs aside to ensure their survival.

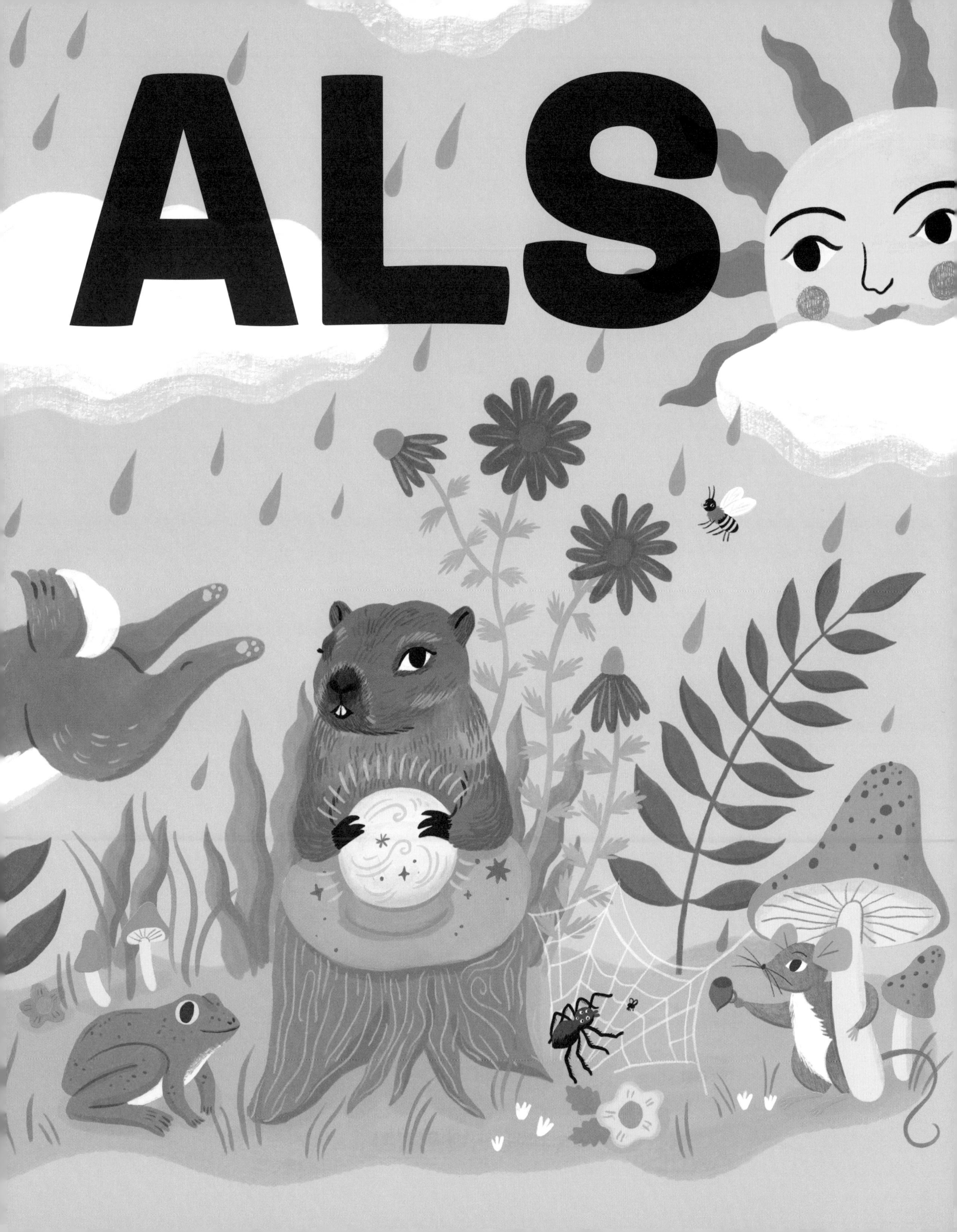
ALS

Cats

Does your cat strut with an air of superiority or sneak around like an undercover spy? Felines have long been viewed as magical and secretive, so naturally, a lot of beliefs and superstitions have developed around them.

HOW DID THAT START? UNLUCKY BLACK CAT

The most common cat superstition is the fear of a black cat crossing your path. In ancient Egypt and ancient China, cats of all colors were honored as goddesses. But in the Middle Ages, Europeans started associating black cats with evil. Back then, many people believed in witches—and we're not talking about the cute, Halloween-y ones. They feared witches kept black cats as companions and could even transform into black cats themselves. That's why a black cat crossing your path was thought to be a sign of bad things to come. Centuries later, when the Puritans traveled across the ocean to the soon-to-be United States, they brought their fear of black cats with them. Sadly, black cats in the US still haven't shaken this bad reputation and are less likely to be adopted at animal shelters. Purr-haps you want to rescue an adorable black feline friend?

LUCKY or UNLUCKY? It all depends...

LUCKY
✳ Black cat on a boat
✳ One white hair on a black cat

UNLUCKY
✳ Meeting a black cat in the early morning
✳ Hearing a black cat cry before leaving on a journey

When it comes to a black cat crossing your path, the world can't agree! It's lucky in Japan and the United Kingdom but unlucky in India, Egypt, and the United States.

Weather Report
It's sure to rain if a cat...
- sneezes
- licks its tail
- washes behind its ears
- looks out the window a lot

Cat Got Your Tongue?
Think twice before sharing secrets with your cat in the room. In the Netherlands, cats are believed to be real gossips!

You've Got To Be Kitten!
In southern Europe, if a cat jumps across your grave, it's believed you'll come back to life as a vampire.

Sneeze The Day
Ka-ching! In Italy, hearing a cat sneeze brings good luck... or even lots of *soldi* (that's Italian for "money").

Whiskers And Weddings
Long ago in the Ozark Mountains of the United States, if you weren't sure whether to accept a marriage proposal, you'd place three hairs from a cat's tail onto a piece of paper, fold it, and tuck it under your doorstep. The next morning, you'd unfold the paper to see what letter the hairs had formed themselves into: a "Y" for "yes" or "N" for "no."

CHARMED!
MANEKI NEKO

A *Maneki Neko* ("beckoning cat") is a Japanese lucky charm often placed at the entrances to businesses and restaurants to bring good fur-tune. The colors of the waving cats have different meanings. A black *Maneki Neko* is for protection, a pink one brings love, and a green one promises good grades in school.

Dogs

With their unshakable loyalty and keen senses, dogs have long been trusty companions. That's probably why most canine superstitions are so paw-sitive.

Lucky Dog!

THANK YOUR LUCKY PAWS IF...

★ You see a white dog before noon
★ You meet three white dogs together
★ You spot a Dalmatian
★ A dog follows you home

Furever Friend

In Scotland, if a strange dog—hello, puppy!—wanders into your house, you'll soon make a new friend.

Ulti-mutt Wave

Some surfers in California say barking like a dog when you spot a huge swell will bring waves of good luck!

STEP RIGHT UP

Stepping in dog poo—eww! Guess what? This is actually lucky in France, but only if it's with your left foot. If it's with your right foot, it just stinks!

HOWL YOU DOIN'?

Has your dog ever growled at something you couldn't see or howled at an empty corner of the room? It may very well have been a ghost! Many people believe dogs have the power to detect supernatural beings. Spooooooky!

SCIENCE CHECK-IN: Does your dog see ghosts? Since we can't understand dog barks, there's no telling for sure what your howling pooch senses. However, scientists do know that a dog's nose is up to 100,000 times more sensitive than ours. Dogs can also hear high frequencies up to four times the distance you can. So your doggy may be catching a whiff of a rodent scurrying in the walls or tuning in to a far-off siren. What do you think?

CANINE WEATHER REPORT
Bad weather's heading your way if your dog:
💧 hangs out under a table
💧 scratches, scratches, scratches
💧 eats grass

AAAH-OOOOH!

Groundhog Day

HOW DID THAT START?
GROUNDHOG DAY

The popular US superstition about the famous
furry forecaster goes like this: On February 2,
if the groundhog comes out of his burrow and
sees his shadow, he'll get scared and dash back
underground, and that means six more weeks of
winter. If he doesn't see his shadow, he'll hang
out under the cloudy skies—you need sunlight
to cast a shadow—and spring is coming early.

YES SHADOW = LONG WINTER
NO SHADOW = EARLY SPRING

This superstition started thousands of years ago with the
Celts—people from modern-day Ireland, Scotland, and parts
of England and France. When February came and the winter
food supply had gotten low, Celtic farmers itched to plant
new crops. February 1 and 2—often the halfway point between
the winter solstice and spring equinox—became their weather
predicting days. A bright sunny sky signaled a cold front on
the way, making the soil too hard to plant. Clouds and rain
foretold an early thaw that could soften the soil.

A badger was brought into the weather predicting process
by the Germans in the Middle Ages. They declared that if
a badger saw its shadow on February 2, they'd be in for six
more weeks of winter. When German immigrants moved to
Pennsylvania in the 1800s, they brought the superstition
with them, but not the badger. Instead, they gave the glory
to the groundhog.

Punxsutawney Phil—the superstar groundhog meteorologist—lives in his burrow at Gobbler's Knob in Punxsutawney, Pennsylvania. His full name is Punxsutawney Phil, Seer of Seers, Sage of Sages, Prognosticator of Prognosticators, and Weather-Prophet Extraordinary. The first official Groundhog Day was in 1887, and every year since, crowds gather to watch Phil do his thing. So, how good is Phil at his job? We're sad to report that he only gets it right about 39 per cent of the time. That's a worse success rate than calling a coin flip! Ouch!

Other Small Mammals

As early civilizations watched small, furry animals scurry about and burrow into the earth, they must have wondered why these creatures were in such a hurry, where they were going, and what happened underground. So many questions = so many superstitions!

RABBIT RULES

In the United Kingdom and the United States, be sure to say "rabbit rabbit"* or "white rabbits" as soon as you wake up in the morning on the first day of the month. Doing this is said to bring good luck for the next 30 days. Did you forget? Just say "tibbar tibbar"—that's "rabbit" backward—right before you go to bed that night.
* Some people repeat rabbit three times.

LUCKY or UNLUCKY? It all depends...

LUCKY
* A chipmunk near your house
* Squirrels doing pretty much anything
* A white rat

UNLUCKY
* A mouse in the house
* A flying bat
* A rabbit crossing your path (but some people also believe this to be good luck!)

Gnaw On This!

Sailors believed rats deserting a ship meant their voyage was doomed. **SCIENCE CHECK-IN:** Rats, like all of us, are not fans of drowning. They often lived in the deepest, darkest places on a ship, and if their beds were wet, they'd hightail it out of there. Even rats know that water in a ship is never a good thing!

Beware Of The Weasel

According to an ancient Greek superstition, a weasel was really a jealous bride who had shape-shifted and was out to destroy the wedding dresses of other brides. Vicious!

DEAR MOUSE

Need to get a bunch of mice or rats out of your house? Write the rodents a letter! An old superstition promises a polite note will do the trick. Make sure your handwriting is neat and suggest a spot they'd enjoy more. Then, fold the note into a tiny square and push it into the mouse hole.

DEAR MOUSE

Horses

Before bikes and cars, horses were a human's most reliable way of getting from one place to another. Riders did everything in their power to make sure their horse was happy and healthy, including saddling them with a host of superstitions.

HORSE SENSE OR NONSENSE?

★ The bigger the ears, the smarter the horse.

★ A horse with eye wrinkles will be a good jumper.

★ When braiding a horse's mane, make an even number of plaits, including the forelock, for luck.

★ If you want a good journey, ride a horse that snorts a lot!

RECIPE FOR A WISH
In the United States, if you meet a white horse, lick your thumb, press it in the palm of your hand then stamp it with your fist and make a wish.

HOW DID THAT START? LUCKY HORSESHOE

Have you ever seen a horseshoe nailed above a doorway for good luck? Which way was it hanging? Some cultures say the two ends should face up in a U-shape to collect the luck inside the shoe. Others vote the ends should point down so fortune rains upon anyone passing underneath it. Either way, it's believed the luck is way more powerful if you find the horseshoe instead of buying it. Possible origins of this old superstition include:

◡ Horseshoes are crescent-shaped, and a crescent moon was thought to be lucky

◡ Horseshoes used to be made of iron, which Western Europeans once viewed as magical because it could withstand fire

◡ A horseshoe has seven holes, and seven is a lucky number in some cultures

CHARMED! DALA HORSE

The Dala horse—or *Dalahäst*—is a good luck charm from Sweden. The red-painted wooden figurine was first carved centuries ago as a child's toy, but today it symbolizes wisdom, strength, and good fortune.

Rituals For The Win

Galloping across the finish line relies on a lot of good luck, so jockeys and racehorse owners often hold tight to the reins of superstition!

★ Never have peanuts in the barn

★ Never take pictures before a race

★ Never name your horse after a family member

★ Either rub your new helmet and silks—that's the colorful uniform jockeys wear for a race—on the ground before wearing them, or never let your helmet and silks touch the ground to avoid a fall. You choose!

RHYME TIME

"One white foot, buy a horse;
Two white feet, try a horse;
Three white feet, look well about him;
Four white feet, do without him."
This old superstition mistakenly thought a horse could be judged by its socks—that's the white or black hair at the bottom of its legs.

Call Me Twinkletoes... Forever

It's considered unlucky to change a horse's name, so choose wisely!

Horsin' Around

If you find a horse with knots and twists in its mane or tail in the morning, pixies or elves may have visited and ridden it during the night!

Other Large Mammals

Many superstitions revolve around keeping farm animals healthy and protecting livestock. But wild animals—especially those looked upon with wonder or confusion—also attract some surprising beliefs.

TRUNK UP OR DOWN?

In Thailand and India, you'll often find elephant ornaments in homes. But which way should the elephant's trunk point to bring wealth, wisdom, and long life? Some say up, but others say down.

LUCKY or UNLUCKY? It all depends...

LUCKY
* Carrying one hair from a goat's beard
* Crossing the path of a single fox
* Seeing a donkey

UNLUCKY
* Dreaming about pigs
* Seeing a white fox
* Seeing a hedgehog (although the ancient Egyptians believed they were good luck!)

Do, re, milk!
It was once believed singing while milking cows would cause their milk to stop flowing. But recent research shows that cows love moo-sic, and when they listen to slow jams, they actually produce more milk!

CHARMED! LUCKY PIG

A *Glücksschwein* is a lucky pig in Germany and Switzerland. Back in the Middle Ages, owning a pig meant you could feed your family during a long, cold winter. Today, marzipan pigs are given on New Year's to bring good fortune.

FOUR-LEGGED WEATHER REPORT

"When sheep gather in a huddle, tomorrow will have a puddle."

"When hogs squeal, romp, and play, expect snow by the end of the day."

"When a cow tries to scratch its ear, a shower is very near."

It's also said that when a cow lies down in the pasture in the morning, rain's on its way. **SCIENCE CHECK-IN:** Some scientists reason that cows stand when it's hot and lie down when it's cooler as a way to regulate their body temperature—the same way you snuggle in bed when you're chilly and kick off the blankets when it's warm. Since it's often cooler before a storm, this bovine belief may stand up. Except... cows lie down just to chew their cud and rest, making it equally possible it's udder nonsense.

WHEN SUPERSTITIONS TURN DANGEROUS

With its long curved snout and sticky 2 ft (0.6 m) long tongue, the giant anteater is seen as a trickster who brings bad luck in South and Central America. As a result, it's been hunted and hit by cars and is now close to being endangered. Pretty sad, especially since giant anteaters are the best exterminators ever—they can eat up to 30,000 ants and termites a day!

Fish

Heads Up!

Many cultures celebrate the new year by eating a fish head.

Some observant Jewish people eat the head of a fish on the first night of Rosh Hashanah. The tradition is a reminder to be a leader and not a follower and to "think with your head, not your tail" during the new year.

At a Chinese New Year meal, the head of a fish is positioned on the table facing toward the most important guest, who is usually the eldest. Because the Chinese word for fish is "*yu*"—which sounds like the word for "surplus"— whoever eats the head should leave some behind to ensure a surplus of food in the year ahead.

IN MY WAKE

Sailors and pirates feared something bad would happen if three sharks followed their ship. Others say one shark following is bad luck, but we're not sure the exact number matters!

GONE FISHIN'

Anglers have a lot of "reel" superstitions when it comes to landing a big catch...

If someone asks "How many fish have you caught so far?" then you won't catch any more.

If you spit on your bait, then you'll catch a lot of fish.

If you go fishing every day, then the fish will stop biting because you're being greedy.

If you throw back your first catch, then you'll catch lots of fish.

SOUNDS FISHY

Carp is a Christmas mealtime tradition in Slovakia, Poland, the Czech Republic, and other eastern European countries. The fish's silvery scales are often tucked under plates or the tablecloth to bring good fortune to the house. Carrying the scales in your wallet is said to attract money for the rest of the year. Fun fact: Before landing on the dinner table, a carp sometimes did laps in a family's bathtub for a few days!

Fish You Were Here

In Trinidad and Tobago, legend has it that no matter where you are in the world, if you eat a cascadoux fish—a type of freshwater catfish—you will be lucky enough to return to beautiful Trinidad to live out the rest of your days.

Make A Fishy Face

According to an old French-Canadian superstition, if a pregnant person craves fish, they better eat some fast, or their baby will be born with a fish head!

CHARMED! KOI

The upstream-swimming, orange-red koi and the humble goldfish are both believed to bring good fortune and happiness in China and Japan. Many people have koi ponds or fishbowls at home. But a fish charm works swimmingly too!

Reptiles And Amphibians

Reptiles and amphibians have been some of our most misunderstood animals because of how they look, transform, and defend themselves. Humans still can't agree if they are good luck or should be feared.

LEAPIN' LIZARDS

You're sitting at the kitchen table when, suddenly, a house lizard lands on your head. Do you scream or cheer? In India and some African countries, a lizard dropping on your head or face is said to bring wealth. But in Thailand, a house lizard on your head bodes a not-so-good day.

Tail In My Shoe

Before science came along and explained a lizard's amazing ability to regenerate its tail, this process was viewed as magical. One lucky lizard superstition says that if you find the tail of a green lizard, put it in your right shoe, and you'll attract happiness and wealth.

Tortoise Tales

Many cultures view the slow, deliberate, and long-living tortoise as wise and strong. In South Africa, having a pet tortoise is often thought to be lucky. But in China and Vietnam, having a pet tortoise is believed to slow down your progress in school or at work.

Go Slow

Helping a turtle cross the road brings good luck, and it's the kind thing to do!

Okey-Croaky

Have you ever heard that touching a toad will give you warts? **SCIENCE CHECK-IN:** Nope—won't happen! Sure, toads have bumpy skin that helps to camouflage them. But those aren't actual warts. Human warts are caused by a virus that only humans can pass on.

THE FROGGY FORECAST

The louder frogs croak, the more rain will fall.
SCIENCE CHECK-IN: Herpetologists (scientists who study reptiles and amphibians) report there actually may be something to this belief. Male frogs croak to attract a mate, and because frogs need water to breed, many of them can sense the drop in barometric pressure before it rains and so they start to croak.

GOODNIGHT HISS

Zzzzzz... In some cultures, dreaming about a snake means a life-changing event is about to happen. Makes sense, as snakes are known for shedding their old skin and growing a new one!

TOAD-ALLY!

Keep a jumping frog in your wallet—an origami frog, that is. In Japanese, the word for frog is "*kaeru*," which also means "to return." An origami frog will cause whatever money you spend to hop right back to you.
Let's go s-hopping!

Birds

Long ago, some people believed birds soared between heaven and earth as messengers of the gods. They'd closely observe every flutter, flap, and tweet, leading to a flock of feathered superstitions.

Don't Look Up!

Did a bird just poop on your head? Ewww... wait, change that to yay! In Turkey, a bird splatting on you means fabulous things are coming your way. In Russia, one bird pooping on you or your car is very lucky, but two birds pooping at the same time doubles the luck (and the poop)! According to the US National Weather Service, a person has a 1-in-15,300 chance of getting struck by lightning in their lifetime, but it has been calculated that they have a 1-in-5,000,000 chance of getting pooped on by a bird!

For the Birds

If your stomach is empty when you hear the cuckoo's first song in spring, you won't have a good year. Long ago, people in Scotland would keep a biscuit under their pillow and take a bite before getting up, just in case the cuckoo called before they had breakfast!

CAN'T STOP RAVEN

If the six ravens living in the Tower of London fly away, the building, the British royal family, and the United Kingdom will collapse. Whoa—that old superstition is intense! For centuries, monarchs have made sure to keep six black-feathered scavengers at the Tower at all times. That's a lot easier today since the ravens now get their wings clipped so they can't stray too far!

COCK-A-DOODLE-DOO!

Hearing a rooster crow...
as you leave for school = it's going be a good day.
in the early evening = bad weather tomorrow.
from a certain direction = a visitor will arrive from that way.

Whooo Said That?

In Uganda and Kenya, seeing an owl is bad luck. An Egyptian superstition says if you see an owl or hear it hoot, bad news is coming. Here's an easy fix—stay out of the woods at night!

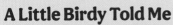

A Little Birdy Told Me

Eating chicken feet will give you bad handwriting.

Fear The Feathers

In Ireland, it was believed if you tucked blackbird feathers under someone's pillow, they'd tell you their deepest secrets.

Caw On In!

In Pakistan, the cawing of a crow near your house means a visitor will arrive soon.

RHYME TIME

"One for sorrow,
Two for joy,
Three for a girl,
Four for a boy,
Five for silver,
Six for gold,
Seven for a secret never to be told."

When you meet a black-and-white magpie in the UK, it's all about the number.

So what if you spot only one magpie? You should give the lone bird a salute or flap your arms and pretend you're also a magpie to increase the number to two!

In other parts of the world, a solo magpie is mag-nificent. A single magpie in South Korea means you'll have a visitor soon, and in China it's good luck.

Insects

Have you ever thought about squishing a creepy crawly? You might want to press the pause button on that, because killing pretty much any insect is universally believed to bring swarms of bad luck.

Buzzy Bee-lief
A hive of bees is the luckiest gift to give. We know that's exactly what you wanted for your birthday!

YOU'RE SO FLY

If a fly lands or crawls on your nose, you will get important news.

If a bee lands or crawls on your head, you will grow up to be great.

If a cricket lands or crawls on your hearth or kitchen, you will have good luck.

HOW DID THAT START?
GO TELL IT TO THE BEES

Back when most people lived on farms, they relied on honey to bake sweet treats. Honey is made by busy and, it seems, happy bees. That's why many European and American beekeepers believed that the hive must be told about all family events. If the bees weren't treated like part of the family, their feelings would be hurt and they'd stop making honey. So, bee kind, leave them a slice of birthday cake, and show off your school spelling bee trophy!

SHINE A LIGHT: FIREFLY MATH

One firefly in the house = an unexpected visitor tomorrow.
Two fireflies in the house = someone inside will marry soon.
Several fireflies in the house = there's glowing to be a party!

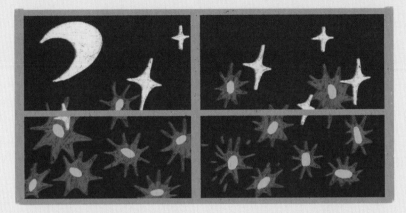

COUNT YOUR LUCKY SPOTS

Ladybugs have long been considered super lucky. Why? Because they feast on small insects that can destroy crops. If a loveable ladybug lands on you, start counting. The number of spots it has can predict the number of happy months ahead, the number of children you'll have, or the amount of money you'll find. Some people believe the redder the ladybug, the greater the luck.

WIGGLY WEATHER PREDICTOR?

According to a superstition in the United States, each of the 13 segments on the fuzzy body of the woolly bear caterpillar corresponds to a week in winter. If a segment is light brown, that means the weather that week will be mild. But if it is black, pull on your mittens, because the week will be chilly. **SCIENCE CHECK-IN:** Scientists have declared this superstition false. The caterpillar's age, the amount of time they've been feeding, and moisture levels in the area all impact its color.

Waiter, There's A Fly In My Soup
If a fly lands inside the glass you're drinking from or on the food you're about to eat, you'll have good fortune. Yum!

Beetle Boost
In Peru, finding an overturned beetle and flipping it back over is believed to bring good luck.

Buggy Weather Report

- If the ant hills are high in July, the winter will be snowy.
- When ladybugs swarm, expect a day that's warm!

Spiders

Spiders help us by catching pesky flies in the incredible, intricate webs they weave. And all over the world, spiders are linked with wealth, creativity, friendship, and good fortune.

POCKET SPIDER

In the United Kingdom, Hungary, and the Caribbean, if a spider crawls into your pocket or you pull one out of your hair—yuck!—it's believed you'll always have money. The bigger the spider, the bigger the stack of bills!

Weaving A Friendship Web
If you accidentally walk into a spider's web, it's believed you'll make a new friend.

WARDROBE WEAVER

If you see a spider spinning its web, expect new clothes soon. Something silky, of course!

RHYME TIME: SPIDER

Be sure to check the clock when you encounter an eight-legged friend!

"A spider in the morning is a sign of sorrow,
A spider at noon brings worry for tomorrow,
A spider in the afternoon is a sign of a gift,
But a spider in the evening will all hopes uplift."

I Spy Mail

Spotted a spider on your door? Check your mailbox. A Russian superstition says a letter is on its way!

Dropping In For Revenge

In Sweden and Finland, if you dare to kill a spider, it will surely rain the next day.

A Tangled Web

A spider in the morning is good luck in Japan. But if you see one at night, a thief may be heading your way!

SUPER SPIDER SENSES

Oh no! Have your cows wandered off the farm? According to an old US superstition, you should find a daddy longlegs—which is sometimes considered a spider and sometimes not—and ask, "Granddaddy, where did my cows go?" and the spider will lift a leg and point in the direction they went.

THE
NATU
WOR

Our ancestors marveled at how colorful flowers, towering trees, sweet fruits, crisp veggies, and glittering gemstones all started deep underground. Such intense beauty just had to be infused with special powers, right? They also spent a lot of time looking up. Will it rain? Which direction is the wind blowing? With no apps or satellites to predict the weather, people turned their eyes to the clouds. And when the Sun set, they studied the twinkling stars and glowing moon in hopes of some guidance down here on Earth—or, at the very least, the granting of a wish (or two).

RAL
LD

Flowers And Plants

GROW! NOW!

The ancient Greeks and Romans believed yelling loudly and angrily at a basil plant would make it grow taller and stronger.

Beware The Succulent

Some believe that keeping a spiky plant, such as a cactus, inside your home invites arguments and sharp words. But if you place it by the entryway or in a window, it will act as your prickly protector.

Be Odd!

Thinking of giving someone flowers? (Aww, you're so nice!) Be sure to give them an odd number. In many countries, an even number of flowers is only for funerals.

RED HOT

It's said that planting peppers when you're angry will make the peppers hotter. Yikes!

LUCKY or UNLUCKY?
It all depends...

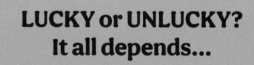

LUCKY
* White heather
* Sunflowers
* Orchids

UNLUCKY
* A single daffodil
* Letting a rose or rose petal touch the floor
* Gifting a potted plant to someone who's sick

FLOWER POWER

In Hawai'i and Tahiti, legend says that if you throw your *lei* into the ocean and it returns to the shore, you're destined to visit the islands again. Just be sure to remove the lei's string before tossing the flowers in the water—the string can strangle turtles and other sea life.

You Butter Believe It

Important question: Do you like butter? Hold a buttercup under your chin. If it gives your skin a golden glow, it means you most certainly do! **SCIENCE CHECK-IN:** The real reason your chin looks yellowish is because buttercups have super glossy petals that reflect light. The shiny petals attract bees and other passing pollinators.

RECIPE FOR A WISH

It's long been believed that dandelions can grant wishes and even predict the future!

How to Wish on a Dandelion

1. Find a dandelion that has turned into a white puff ball. This is important, because yellow ones won't work.

2. Blow the seed head—the white puff ball—while making a wish. If you blow off all the seeds in one breath, your wish will come true.

3. Want to know how many kids you'll have someday? Just count the seeds that remain or the number of puffs it takes to blow them all away.

Four-Leaf Clovers

HOW DID THAT START?
FOUR-LEAF CLOVER

The four-leaf clover is a symbol of good luck around the world. But if you've ever searched your backyard or a field looking for one, you'll know how tricky they are to find. Some people believe Celtic priests called Druids kickstarted the clover's fame in the early days of Ireland. Druids supposedly carried a clover to shoo away spirits, while children in the Middle Ages believed they'd be able to see fairies if they kept one in their pocket!

Hope

Faith

Did you know each of the four leaves has a meaning?

Luck

Love

Have you heard about the "luck of the Irish" and seen pictures of leprechauns holding shamrocks? A shamrock actually only has three leaves, not four.

How To Find A Four-Leaf Clover In Four Easy Steps

Step 1
Stand by the edge of a clover patch.

Step 2
A section containing 10,000 clovers is about the size of an average car tire. Begin with this small section, but do NOT examine the 10,000 clovers one by one— that would take forever!

Step 3
Instead, gaze about without focusing on any individual clover. Allow your eyes to naturally find the odd one out. Hint: A three-leaf clover has a triangular shape, and a four-leaf clover looks square.

Step 4
If you don't find one, move on to a different patch. Some patches don't have any. If you do find one, mark the spot. Usually you'll discover a bunch more in the same area. Good luck!

It is said that if you give your four-leaf clover to someone else, your luck will double.

Trees

AGE-CORN

Do your parents or grandparents complain about growing old? Hand them an acorn! A British superstition says that carrying an acorn in your pocket will keep you forever young. **SCIENCE CHECK-IN:** Nope—acorns don't have the power to turn back the clock. This superstition probably started because mighty oak trees live for a long, long time yet grow from a tiny acorn seed.

Acorn Of Protection

Place a single acorn on your windowsill to keep lightning away. This old Scandinavian belief has roots in a Norse myth about Thor—the god of thunder—who found shelter from a storm under an oak tree.

Tree Of Truth

It's impossible to tell a lie if you're standing or sitting under a linden tree, according to an ancient German superstition. Not that you'd ever do such a thing, of course...

FAIRY RESPECT

In Irish folklore, a lone hawthorn tree in the middle of a field is home to fairies, and any person who tries to cut the tree down will suffer misfortune for the rest of their days. There's a golf club in Belfast in Northern Ireland with a fairy tree growing on the golf course, and any golfer who hits it with their ball must immediately apologize to the tree.

HOW DID THAT START?
KNOCKING ON WOOD

Knocking on or touching wood is like a protection charm against something bad happening. Many people believe that if things are going well or if they voice their hopes or boast, they will be jinxed, and everything will be ruined. Knocking on wood is thought to reverse the jinx. A popular theory is that this superstition began with the ancient pagan religions that believed helpful spirits lived inside trees. By touching a tree, you were letting the spirits know that you knew they were there. In return, the spirits would make sure all went OK for you. Knocking on a tree trunk soon became knocking on wooden furniture. Now, people often just say "knock wood" or "touch wood," and the tree spirits get the idea.

★ In Sweden, say "peppar, peppar ta i trä"— "pepper, pepper touch wood"—after knocking for extra luck
★ In Brazil and Portugal, you must knock three times
★ In Italy, you get luck by touching iron, because iron lasts longer than wood

PEPPAR, PEPPAR TA I TRÄ

RECIPE FOR A WISH

See a leaf falling from a tree? Catch it before it touches the ground! If you do, the wish you make will come true.

Fruits And Vegetables

RECIPE FOR A WISH

Stick a watermelon seed to your forehead. Quick—make a wish before it falls off!

A-PEELING BELIEFS

If you eat a peach, you'll be granted a long life.

If you cut a banana, you'll have bad luck. Break it with your fingers instead.

If you feast on a cabbage, you'll attract wealth or silver coins.

FOR THE ZEST DAY

Place nine lemons in a bowl for good luck and happiness. Not eight or 10—got it?

And They Lived Pine-apply Ever After

In Singapore, rolling a pineapple into your new house before stepping in yourself allows good fortune to roll in too. Sweet!

Love Is The Pits

Prick holes in an orange, tuck it under your armpit, and sleep with it there all night. In the morning, offer it to the person you really like. If they eat it, they'll become your sweetheart.

SOUR & SPICY

Many shops and homes in India hang seven chilies and a lemon from a thread on the door. It's an old superstition meant to keep away Alakshmi, the goddess of misfortune. She likes eating sour and hot things, so if she's happy with the treat, it's believed she won't enter to bring bad luck.
SCIENCE CHECK-IN: This is actually a supersmart natural pesticide. When the cotton thread pierces the chilies and lemon, a pungent and sour odor is slowly released, and this stench helps to repel flies and mosquitoes.

HOW DID THAT START?
CARROTS = GOOD EYESIGHT

Have you ever heard that eating carrots will help you see in the dark? Carrots do contain beta-carotene that definitely helps to keep your eyes healthy, but the orange veggie won't give you magic night vision. It seems this superstition can be traced back to the United Kingdom during World War II. In 1940, a Royal Air Force pilot was the first to shoot down a German plane in the dark of night using new secret radar technology. But the British didn't want the Germans to know they had this new weapon, so they told reporters their pilots' night vision superpower was the result of eating lots and lots of carrots. Suddenly, articles appeared in all the newspapers championing carrots. It's unknown if the Germans fell for the trick, but adults sure believed it, and carrots began appearing in kids' lunch boxes!

Birthstones

Birthstones are colorful gemstones mined from the earth or formed inside an oyster. Each one is connected with one of the 12 months of the year. To find your birthstone, all you need to know is your birthday. Wearing your special birthstone is believed to invite happiness, health, and good fortune.

January = garnet

Brilliant belief: Travelers in ancient Rome and ancient China often carried garnets for protection. Eastern Asiatic warriors and Aztec warriors in Central America would bring them into battle.

February = amethyst

Brilliant belief: It was once believed that sleeping with an amethyst under your pillow kept bad dreams away.

MARCH = AQUAMARINE

Brilliant belief: Early sailors would wear aquamarine charms etched with a picture of the Roman god Neptune—who ruled the seas—to protect against danger and seasickness.

A REAL GEM!

Some historians date birthstones all the way back to the Bible. Moses instructed that his brother Aaron's breastplate—the thing soldiers strapped onto their chests to protect their heart in battle—should have 12 precious gemstones each representing the 12 tribes of Israel. Many years later, a guy named Flavius Josephus connected the idea of the 12 gemstones with the 12 signs of the zodiac. People in Europe and the Middle East spent the next thousand or so years carrying around gems as lucky charms, rotating them with the changing zodiac. Flash forward to 1870 in the United States when the jewelry store Tiffany & Co. came up with a great way to encourage people to buy their friends and family jewelry for their birthdays—birthstones! They wrote a pamphlet that paired gems with the months of the year instead of with the zodiac. The National Association of Jewelers jumped on board, and in 1912, they created an official list that was shared with every jewelry store in the US.

April = diamond

Brilliant belief: In ancient India, it was believed that diamonds were formed when bolts of lightning struck rocks, so people reasoned that wearing a diamond prevented them from being struck by lightning.

The real deal: Diamonds are formed deep underground when the element carbon experiences extreme pressure and tremendously high temperatures.

May = emerald

Brilliant belief: Many ancient civilizations believed that wearing an emerald would reveal hidden truths and let you predict the future.

JUNE = PEARL

Brilliant belief:
According to an ancient Chinese legend, pearls formed inside the head of a dragon, and the dragon then carried them between its teeth. The only way to get your hands on the pearls—if you were brave enough—was to slay the dragon, and then the pearls would give you wisdom.
The real deal: Pearls are formed inside oysters and other mollusks.

July = ruby

Brilliant belief: Ancient Burmese warriors believed the gem made them invincible in battle.

August = peridot

Brilliant belief: Peridot appears to glow from within, so the gem was believed to chase away nightmares—kind of like a natural nightlight!

September = sapphire

Brilliant belief: It was once believed sapphires guarded against poisoning.

October = opal

Brilliant belief: Opals are considered lucky by Eastern cultures, but Western cultures often believed only those born in October should wear them. Otherwise, you'll have bad luck.

November = topaz

Brilliant belief: The ancient Romans believed topaz improved eyesight, and the ancient Egyptians wore it in jewelry to protect them from injury.

December = turquoise

Brilliant belief: In the Middle East and Europe, turquoise was once used as a good luck charm for horses and riders, protecting both from a fall.

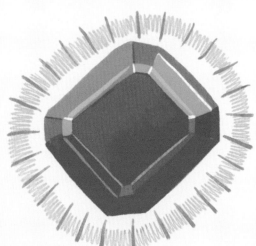

Rain

RECIPE FOR A WISH
When you see a bolt of lightning flash across the sky, make a wish.

LOOKS LIKE... RAIN
In Colombia, if storm clouds gather in the sky, you should quickly place a mirror on the ground. If the sky sees how ugly it looks, it'll turn its frown upside down and not rain.

Thunderpants
In the United States, it's said that if a snapping turtle bites your toe or finger, it won't let go until it hears a clap of thunder. Ouch!

Monkey Wedding
If it rains while the Sun is shining in South Africa, people say that a monkey is getting married. In Nigeria and Côte d'Ivoire, it's said a lion cub is being born.

NO-NO YO-YO!
The Prime Minister of Syria banned yo-yos in 1933 because it was believed playing with them caused a severe drought. Why? A yo-yo goes down but returns to your hand before touching the ground. Could the yo-yo be making the rain do the same thing? True story: The day after the ban came into force, it rained! The yo-yo ban has since been lifted.

RHYMES & REASONS

"Oak before ash, we're in for a splash. Ash before oak, we're in for a soak."

Oak and ash trees in the United Kingdom compete every spring to see which will open their leaves first. If the oak wins the race, farmers believe a dry summer with little rain will follow. **SCIENCE CHECK–IN:** Trees are not great fortune tellers. When an oak tree's leaves bud and bloom depends on spring temperatures. When an ash tree blooms depends on day length and sunlight. But neither can accurately predict what will happen in the summer.

"Red sky at night, sailor's delight. Red sky in morning, sailor's warning."

SCIENCE CHECK–IN:
There's some truth to this ancient saying.
First thing to know: When the sky looks red, it means the Sun is illuminating the underside of the clouds.
Second thing: The Sun rises in the east and sets in the west.
Third thing: In most of North America, Europe, Asia, and the Middle East, weather usually moves from west to east.
Now to put it all together: A red sky at sunset means the Sun is illuminating *departing* clouds to the east, so clear skies tomorrow look likely. A red sky at sunrise means the Sun is illuminating clouds *approaching* from the west, so best to bring an umbrella today.

"If birds fly low, expect rain and a blow."

SCIENCE CHECK–IN: Can birds predict "fowl" weather? It seems so! Most birds have a Vitali organ. This is a special receptor in their middle-ear that can sense a drop in atmospheric pressure, and that drop means a storm is on its way.

Rainbows

Imagine you lived thousands of years ago and you're going about your day when you glance up and—whoa! As if by magic, brilliant colors glimmer in an arch across the sky. Is it any wonder awesome rainbows were often believed to be a bridge to the heavens, a message from the gods, or a symbol of hope?

WHAT EXACTLY IS A RAINBOW?

An optical illusion, that's what! We see rainbows when sun shines through falling rain. The Sun's light is actually made of different colors. When it hits water droplets, the light bends, splits into different colors, and reflects back, allowing us to see a rainbow.

POT O' GOLD

A popular Irish legend says that at the end of a rainbow you'll find a pot of gold—and a cheeky leprechaun too!

Don't Point!

No matter where you live in the world, it's bad luck to point your finger at a rainbow. Come on—pointing is kind of rude!

Lucky, Lucky

Seeing a double rainbow means you'll be granted double good luck!

RECIPE FOR A WISH

When you see a rainbow, close your eyes and make a wish. Then count to ten while keeping your eyes closed. Open your eyes. If the rainbow is still there, your wish will come true!

SCIENCE CHECK-IN: Can you ever get to the end of a rainbow? A rainbow may look like an arch, but it's actually a full circle! Because we're standing on the ground, the horizon blocks us from seeing the bottom half. Sometimes, pilots in planes or hikers on top of tall mountains can see the full circle, and you might be able to spot it in a fountain or sprinklers. But since a circle has no end, there's no end to a rainbow, so the answer is "no."

Snow

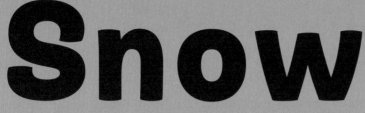

JUST GO INSIDE

If you sit outside on your doorstep and knit during the winter in Iceland, it's said you will cause the icy weather to last months longer.

The Inside Scoop

In the Ozark Mountains in the United States, some people believe persimmons can predict the winter's weather. Split open a locally grown persimmon and take a peek inside the fruit...

Fork shape = mild winter with light, powdery snow

Spoon shape = lots of snow to scoop!

Knife shape = a bitterly cold winter that "cuts like a knife"

Fog Forecaster

In parts of the Appalachian Mountains in the United States, it's believed the number of foggy mornings in August will equal the number of snowfalls that coming winter.

COUNTING SHEEP

If you dream about white sheep in Iceland, expect snow soon. Fun fact: Unlike other sheep, Icelandic sheep have two layers of fleece for double protection against extreme cold.

RECIPE FOR A WISH

In South Korea, a wish on the first snowflake of the first snowfall will come true.

SNOW DAY—HOORAY!!!!

If you live in the northern United States or Canada, you and your friends probably have a special ritual to convince Mother Nature to reward you with a snow day. Here are some ingredients for the perfect How-to-Make-A-Snow-Day recipe. The only problem? We don't know which ones work and in which order. Do you?

✳ Flush one ice cube down the toilet for every inch of snow you desire
✳ Place a white crayon on the windowsill or in the freezer
✳ Yell "Snow Day!" into the freezer, then eat A LOT of ice cream for dinner
✳ Wear mismatched socks to bed
✳ Brush your teeth with your non-dominant hand, and sleep with one sock on
✳ Wear your pajamas both inside out and backward
✳ Sleep with a spoon under your pillow
✳ Sleep with your feet at the top of your bed and your head at the bottom

Moon

LUCKY or UNLUCKY? It all depends...

LUCKY
✳ A full moon on Monday ("Moon day")
✳ Bowing or curtseying three times during a new moon
✳ Picking flowers under the glow of a blue moon

UNLUCKY
✳ Viewing the new moon through a window
✳ Pointing at the moon
✳ Eating or drinking during a lunar eclipse

THE LUNAR WEATHER REPORT

"If a circle forms a halo 'round the moon, 'twill rain soon."

SCIENCE CHECK-IN: Meteorologists report this rhyme is true. That circle around the moon is called a halo. Halos are formed when moonlight bends as it passes through the tiny ice crystals in wispy cirrus clouds. These high, thin clouds often appear before rain showers or storms.

MOON-EY

Want lots of money? According to an old Sicilian superstition, the minute the new moon appears, you say, *"Benvenuta luna che mi porti fortuna!"* ("Welcome, moon and may you bring me good fortune!") while turning over a silver coin in your pocket.

RHYME TIME

"I see the moon, the moon sees me. The moon sees somebody I want to see."

In New England in the US, an old superstition says that you should chant this rhyme followed by the name of the person you wish to see. Then, in a few days, you'll see them!

BENVENUTA LUNA CHE MI PORTI FORTUNA!

IT'S ONLY A PHASE

Farmers in the United States have long looked to the phases of the moon to determine the best time to plant.

🌙 Crops that grow above ground, such as corn, wheat, and cucumbers, should be planted in the light of the moon, or when it's growing fuller (known as waxing). Why? So the bright moonlight can "pull" the plant out of the ground.

🌙 Crops that grow underground, such as potatoes, onions, and carrots, should be planted in the dark of the moon, or when it's growing slimmer (known as waning). Why? So the dim moonlight can "push" the roots deeper into the ground.

RECIPE FOR A WISH
Make a wish on the new moon. But for it to come true, don't look up at the moon again until the next new moon.

Stars

THE STARRY WEATHER REPORT
"When the stars begin to huddle,
the Earth will soon become a puddle."
SCIENCE CHECK-IN: If it's very cloudy
at night, the stars look like they're huddled
together. And the more clouds there are,
the greater the chance of rain.

CHARMED! THE NORTH STAR

Through time, sailors often got tattoos of the
North Star. The North Star was an important
navigating tool, letting sailors in the northern
hemisphere know which way was north so their
ship stayed on course. They believed that having
the lucky star inscribed on their body would
ensure they'd always be brought safely home.

Did you know shooting stars are not stars? They're actually meteors, or space rocks, that we briefly see as they burn up upon entering Earth's atmosphere.

STAR STRUCK

Have you lost your baseball glove or misplaced your library book? Just gaze up at the night sky and count 100 different stars. When you're done, the thing you've lost will be found.

THE BEST WAY TO WISH UPON A SHOOTING STAR

Some people believe you have to make a wish quickly before the flash of light disappears or it won't come true. Others believe you have to wish for someone else, not yourself. Who would you make a wish for?

RECIPE FOR A WISH

If you count nine stars for nine nights, the wish you make will be granted on the ninth night.

RHYME TIME: Have you ever wished upon a star?

"Star light, star bright,
First star I see tonight,
I wish I may, I wish I might,
Have the wish I wish tonight."

This British nursery rhyme was made popular in the Disney movie *Pinocchio*, but the superstition of wishing upon the first star of the evening or on a shooting star goes back to ancient times. The ancient Greek astronomer Ptolemy believed that shooting stars happened when the gods up in the heavens wanted to peek down on Earth, so they pushed aside a star, causing it to fall. He figured this was an excellent moment to ask for a wish, seeing as he had their attention!

Space Travel

When you think about rocket scientists and astronauts, you probably think high-tech, logical, and scientific. But you should also add superstitious—space travel has a slew of out of this world rituals! Imagine sitting atop tons of explosive fuel as you blast into the unknown, and you can understand why even those with nerves of steel are hoping for a dash of luck!

BOOTSTRAPPING IT

Jeff Bezos—the founder of Amazon—wears his lucky cowboy boots every time his human spaceflight startup, Blue Origin, launches a space vehicle. The one time he forgot was the only time a launch failed.

Final Countdown

The US space agency NASA has never numbered a mission 13 again after an oxygen tank exploded on Apollo 13 on April 13.

Around With Clover

The first three SpaceX launches failed, but a lucky four-leaf clover was on the logo patch when the fourth spacecraft—*Falcon I*—orbited Earth in 2008. The clover has appeared on every SpaceX patch since then.

Pass The Popcorn

What do Russian cosmonauts do for good luck the night before a launch? They gather to watch the 1970 adventure movie *White Sun of the Desert*.

Potty Break

On the bus ride to the launch pad, Russian cosmonauts make a stop to pee on the bus's rear right wheel. Yuri Gagarin, who made history in 1961 as the first human to travel into outer space, had his bus halt on the way to the launch pad because he really neeeded to pee! And since it worked for him, cosmonauts keep stopping the bus.

Breakfast Of Champions

No matter the time of day, NASA astronauts always eat eggs and steak before launch. They're paying tribute to the first American astronaut in space, Alan Shepard, who ate this meal before his Mercury Freedom 7 mission in 1961.

Hair, Not There

It's believed to be bad luck for Russian cosmonauts to watch the Soyuz rocket get rolled out to the launch pad. Instead, they're sent to get haircuts.

DEAL ME IN

Before boarding a NASA spacecraft, the astronaut commander sits down with the tech crew for a card game. They must play until the commander loses a hand.

CHARMED! PEANUTS

Inside NASA's Space Flight Operations Facility at the Jet Propulsion Laboratory (JPL) in California, tensions run high during unmanned space launches and landings. All eyes stay fixed on the screens, and all hands reach into jars of peanuts. Yep—the rocket scientists and engineers are munching on peanuts. The superstition started during JPL's Ranger missions in the 1960s. The spacecrafts were built to fly to the moon and take pictures, but the first six Rangers failed during launch or while leaving orbit. On the seventh launch, an engineer shared the peanuts he'd brought for a snack with everyone at mission control, and the mission succeeded. Ever since, launches and landings have been powered by peanuts.

THE HUM BODY

Our bodies are amazing! We breathe, digest, move, solve problems, and love. But how does all that happen? What's actually going on inside us? The workings of our bodies felt even more mysterious to our ancestors than they do to us, and spirits were often blamed for problems. Magic was thought to flow through blood and saliva, hair was associated with strength, and hands were believed to hold great power. On top of that, there were all the odd noises. The way some people sneezed or burped sure sounded as if something supernatural was at work!

Our ancestors would try to puzzle out every itch, tingle, and twinge by comparing experiences. Although not rational, superstitions gave comfort and answers when a doctor wasn't nearby, and web searches weren't yet a thing.

AN

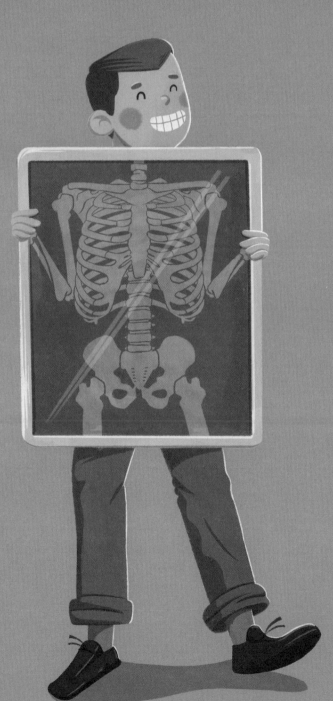
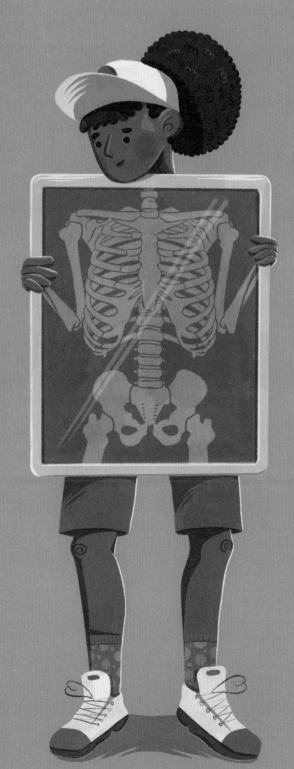

Ears And Eyes

SAY WHAT?

Is your ear tingling, itching, or buzzing? If it's your left ear, it's said someone's saying bad stuff about you. If it's your right ear, they're saying good things. If you want to stop the nasty chatter, either bite your tongue (not too hard!) or smear saliva on your left ear.

SCIENCE CHECK–IN: This superstition is credited to the ancient Roman philosopher Pliny the Elder. But what Pliny didn't know then—but doctors know now—is that ringing or buzzing in your ears is called tinnitus. There's only one way to know if someone's talking behind your back. Ask them... nicely.

HOT PRAISE

If your ears are burning, it's believed someone somewhere is saying super nice stuff about you. That's why people often tell you, "Wow! Your ears must've been burning," when you've been complimented but weren't there to hear the praise. However, in some places, burning ears means not-so-nice stuff is being said about you behind your back!

RECIPE FOR A WISH

If your eyelash falls out, place it on the back of your left hand, make a wish, and press your right palm down over the eyelash. If the eyelash sticks to your palm, your wish will come true.

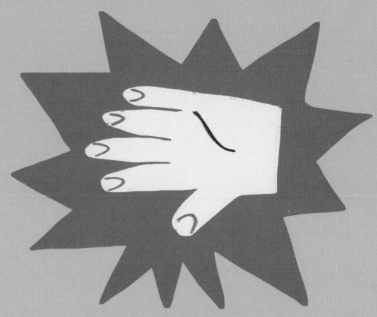

TWITCH AND TELL

Isn't it an odd feeling when your eyelid twitches uncontrollably? Different cultures have different superstitions about what it means.

In Trinidad and India, if your left eye twitches, bad news is coming. If your right eye twitches, expect good news.

In Hawai'i, if your left eye twitches, a stranger is on their way. If your right eye twitches, a baby will be born soon.

In Cameroon and Nigeria, if your lower eyelid twitches, you'll soon cry. If your upper lid twitches, a visitor is on their way.

SCIENCE CHECK-IN: Doctors say twitching often happens if you're tired, stressed, or haven't been drinking enough water.

MYTHBUSTER!

"If you cross your eyes, they'll get stuck that way."
Nope. Not going to happen. Most people's eye muscles let you move your eyes in all directions—and back again.

Forget About It

Did someone catch you doing something you shouldn't have been? In Nigeria, if you put one of your eyelashes in their shoe, they'll forget all about it!

Nose And Mouth

Try this tongue twister: Say "silly superstitions" five times fast!

ON THE TIP OF YOUR TONGUE

If you bite your tongue, it means someone just thought about you. If this happens, quickly think of a number between one and 26. Find the corresponding letter from the alphabet (A=1, B=2, C=3, and so on). Who do you know whose name starts with that letter? That's the person who just thought about you!

Tongue Of Truth

If you bite your tongue while eating, it's believed it's because you've recently told a lie.

Sounds Fishy

An old remedy to make a sore throat feel better is to place a salted herring on your feet or around your neck. Eeeew! We'll stick to cough drops, thanks!

The Nose Knows

If your nose itches, you're about to get into an argument, or someone—often a relative—is about to visit.

GOT A GUSHER?

To cure a nosebleed, it was once believed that you should drape green seaweed across your forehead or wear a dead frog or toad in a silk bag around your neck. What you should really do, according to doctors, is grab a tissue, sit up straight, and pinch the soft part of your nose closed.

HICCUP

In Greece and Russia, hiccups are a sign that someone is thinking about you. To reveal who it is, list out loud all the people you think it could be. The hiccups will stop when you say the correct name.
SCIENCE CHECK-IN: Hiccups happen when your diaphragm—a muscle below your lungs that helps you breathe—has a sudden spasm. This sharp intake of air causes the vocal chords in your throat to close briefly, and you start making the "hic" sound on repeat. Some hiccup culprits are gobbling down food, swallowing too much air, carbonated beverages, excitement, and stress. So while it doesn't mean someone isn't thinking about you, hiccups are more likely to be a sign to take things one bite at a time at the dinner table.

GUARD THE DOOR

Covering your mouth when you yawn is the polite thing to do, but the action comes from a very old superstition. Your hand was there to block spirits from coming out of or going into your open mouth!
SCIENCE CHECK-IN: When you yawn, oxygen goes in and carbon dioxide comes out. Nothing else. Except maybe some bad breath!

Tooth Or Dare

Got a toothache? One superstition says to sit backward on a donkey and another says to kiss the donkey—your choice!

Wisdom Teeth

Want to see your future? Look in a mirror! If your teeth are pushed close together, you will live near your childhood home when you grow up. If your teeth are spaced far apart, you will live far away from your childhood home when you're an adult.

Sneezing

Aaaachoo! Whether it's a tiny sniffle or a snot-spraying explosion, when someone sneezes, we automatically give a blessing or a wish for good health. It doesn't matter if the sneezer is a complete stranger—we still say it. What's up with that? Superstition, of course!

HOW DID THAT START? SAYING SOMETHING AFTER A SNEEZE

Sneezing is kind of odd, isn't it? The way it bursts out of you with no warning and a lot of noise. We now know that sneezes are a way for our bodies to clear out bacteria, viruses, dust, and pollutants. But before science taught us that, sneezes were seen as a warning of something bad. Various ancient cultures believed your soul resided in your head, so a sneeze could pull your soul out through your nose and let evil spirits whoosh in! Offering up a blessing was a way to stop a spirit invasion. Also, without modern medicine, a cold or the flu often had a not-so-happy ending. That's why the ancient Romans would tell a sneezer "*Salve*," which means "good health to you," and the ancient Greeks would wish "long life."

There's another origin story that takes place during the 6th century when the deadly bubonic plague was spreading through Europe. People realized that a sneeze was often a first symptom, so Pope Gregory the Great ordered that everyone should say a short prayer—"God bless you"—when they heard a sneeze. This would then protect both themselves and the sneezer from an untimely end. Today, whether it's out of habit or manners, we still answer every sneeze with a response.

WHAT WE SAY WHERE

Arabic-speaking countries: "*Alhamdulellah!*" (Praise be to God!)
Balkan countries: "*Na zdravie!*" (To health!)
East African countries: "*Afya!*" (Health!)
English-speaking countries: "Bless you!" or "God bless you!"
France: "*À tes souhaits!*" (To your wishes!)
Germany: "*Gesundheit!*" (Health!)
Hawai'i: "*Kihe a mauli ola!*" (Sneeze and live!)
Israel: "*Labriut!*" (For your health!)
Kenya: (said only to kids) "*Kua!*" (Grow!)
Netherlands: (after the third sneeze) "*Morgen mooi weer!*"
(The weather will be nice tomorrow!)
Scandinavian countries: "*Prosit!*" (May it be useful!)
Spanish-speaking countries: "*Salud!*" (Good health!)
Turkey: "*Çok yaşa!*" (Live long!)
Uganda: "*Bbuka!*" (Recover!)
Serbia: (said only to kids) "*Pis maco!*" (Go away, kitten!)
Because cats make noises that sound a bit like a person sneezing!
What do YOU say?

SOME SNEEZY SUPERSTITIONS

In eastern European countries, if someone sneezes while telling you something, they're telling the truth.

In Scotland, some believed that a newborn baby was under a fairy's spell until its first sneeze released it.

In Iceland, Germany, and the southern US, sneezing three times before breakfast is thought to bring a gift!

If your cat sneezes three times, someone in your family will soon catch a cold.

Hair And Fingernails

GIVE IT A CURL

In parts of the United States and United Kingdom, it's said that eating bread crusts makes your hair curly. Do you think this was a tricky way for adults to get kids to eat all their sandwich?

The Full Moon Cut, Please

Want luxurious locks? In many countries, it was once believed that if you cut your hair under a full moon, it would grow back thicker and longer.

Tangled

According to an old North Carolina superstition, if you let a bird use a strand of your hair to build a nest in spring, you'll have headaches in summer. But what a nice, cozy home the bird will have!

It All Rinses Out In The Wash

We declare a no shower day! Washing your hair on the first day of the Lunar New Year is believed to wash away your good luck.

HONEY, I'M HOME!

Hair We Aren't
Trim on a Tuesday? Think again! In India, barbershops used to be closed on Tuesdays because it was considered an unlucky day for a haircut. In Thailand, Wednesday was the no-go haircut day.

Tiny Nibbles
In Wales, it was believed if you cut a baby's fingernails before they were one year old, the baby would grow up to be a thief. Parents would bite them down instead!

RHYME TIME
"Beware of a man,
Be he friend or brother,
Whose hair is one color,
And beard another."

CUT CUT, SNIP SNIP
Sailors often wouldn't cut their hair or nails while at sea, as they were convinced that doing so would cause a storm. Imagine what the crew looked like by the end of a long voyage!

Nailed It
In Turkey, India, and South Korea, trimming fingernails or toenails after dark was once believed to cause early death. Why? Cute little nail clippers didn't exist centuries ago, so sharp knives were used to chop delicate nails. You do the math: darkness + sharp object = ouch! (and lots of blood) ouch! + no medicine = serious infection or death.

Hands And Feet

IT'S NOT RIGHT!

Early civilizations were suspicious of anything different, and this included the use of the left side of the body. The left hand and foot became associated with bad luck, even though so many famous scientists, artists, performers, and world leaders are all proud lefties. Superstitions include:

If your right hand itches, money's coming your way. If your left hand itches, you'll lose money.

If you step out of bed with your left foot first, you'll have a bad day.

You should enter a room with your right foot for good luck. This is where the phrase "put your best foot forward" comes from and why bad dancers are said to have "two left feet."

FINGERS CROSSED

Can you guess one of the most popular emojis in English-speaking countries? Yep—it's the fingers crossed one. For centuries, people have been crossing their index and middle fingers to ask a higher power for hope, help, protection, and even forgiveness. That's why when folks tell a lie, they cross their fingers behind their backs!

On The Other Hand

If you walk by a graveyard or pass a hearse in Japan, people say you should tuck your thumbs in to protect your parents. The Japanese word for "thumb" translates to "parent-finger."

Funny Bone

In Mexico, if you bump your elbow, a surprise is heading your way. Rub away the pain, and the surprise goes away. In the United Kingdom, if you bang one elbow, bang the other one for luck!

HOW DID THAT START? PRESSING THUMBS

Press thumbs to wish someone good luck in Germany and Switzerland. To do it, press your thumbs into the palms of your hands and wrap all your fingers in a fist around your thumbs. Then say, "*Ich drücke dir die Daumen,*" which translates to "I press my thumbs for you." No one knows for sure where this superstition came from, but it may go back to 4th century Rome. In gladiator battles, a thumbs up from the referee signaled the gladiator would face death, while tucked in thumbs let them live. Or it could be because the thumb was considered one of the luckiest fingers. Just think of all the cool things your thumb lets you do!

What's Shakin'?

If you shake your legs in South Korea, it's said you'll shake away all your good luck.

WATCH WHERE YOU'RE GOING!

In cultures around the world, you should never step over someone's legs if they're laying on the floor, as it's believed they'll stop growing. If you do it, immediately step back over to reverse the curse.

Itchin' To Go

If your feet itch in Ghana, it's time to start packing because you're about to travel soon.

RECIPE FOR A WISH

If you stub a toe, it hurts something awful. But look on the bright side—you get to make a wish!

Clothing

INSIDE OUT

In both Hungary and Italy, accidently putting on a piece of clothing inside out is said to bring good luck—but only if you wear it like that until bedtime! The same goes for mismatched socks. Just don't get any sneaky ideas—you don't get luck if you do it deliberately.

Dot, Dot, Dot

In the Philippines and France, wearing clothing with polka dots is said to bring wealth and good fortune because all those small circles look like coins! For even more luck, wear polka dots on New Year's Day.

Wrong Thread

Did you find a stray thread on your clothes? In Finland, that means someone is thinking about you.

On The Mend

Got a hole in your undies? An old superstition says it's bad luck to sew up the hole while you're still wearing the undies (not to mention an accident waiting to happen!).

HOWDY, PARDNER

American cowboys believed it was bad luck to put their hat on their bed. If you think about the head lice and all that dust, you'll understand why!

Many people admit they have a lucky pair of underwear. Do you?

BONKERS ABOUT BUTTONS

If you find a button in the street, then you will soon make a new friend. If you find a button with four holes, you will soon hear good news.

CHARMED! BUTTONS

Some people carry one button in their pocket or bag for good luck. Others collect lots of buttons in a jar to multiply their good luck. Long ago, some fortune tellers would ask a question about your future and then scoop up a handful of buttons. An even number of buttons meant the answer was yes, and an odd number meant no.

Socks And Shoes

Knot For You

Only give a gift of shoes to someone you don't like. In South Korea, gifting shoes is believed to make the recipient run away from you or break the friendship.

Sole-mates

In India, leaving your shoes sole side up means there will soon be a quarrel, and leaving your slippers upside down is considered bad luck in Syria, Egypt, Nepal, and Brazil.

Shoe-perstition

In the United States and the United Kingdom, new shoes should be kept off the table or else they'll bring bad luck. In other countries, the belief is that shoes shouldn't go on the bed.

THE SHOE WEATHER REPORT

In Japan, some kids loosen their sandal or shoe and then kick it up into the air. The way it lands is believed to predict the next day's weather.

- If it lands on its side, the day will be filled with clouds
- If it lands upside down, prepare for a mix of weather
- If it lands on the sole, here comes the sun

LEFT FOR LUCK

In the Appalachian Mountains of the United States, if you find a penny, you're supposed to tuck it in your left shoe for good luck. Some brides do this on their wedding day.

A Hole Note

A hole in your sock means an important letter is coming soon.

SHOELACE SUPERSTITIONS

If you find a knot in your shoelaces, then you're going to have a very lucky day.

If your right shoelace comes untied, then someone is saying good things about you.

If your left shoelace comes untied while you're walking, then someone is gossiping about you.

RECIPE FOR A WISH

If both your socks slip down, make a wish as you pull them up.

IN,

OUT,

ABO

Home, sweet, home! Many of our at-home superstitions and traditions look to sweep away bad energy and cook up a delicious menu of wishes so we feel cozy, happy, and safe. Out and about in the world, we often encounter activities with unpredictable outcomes, and this sometimes makes us feel stressed and confused. That's why when we take a test, sing in the school musical, or step up to the plate to hit a home run, some of us carry a lucky charm or perform a certain ritual. A lot of the time, these quirky things really do make us perform better. Many superstitions give us a sense of hope, and there's absolutely nothing wrong with that! The key is to not trust luck instead of your own logic, because your brain wins. Every time. No contest.

AND

UT

At Home

HOW DID THAT START? UMBRELLAS INDOORS

Around the world, opening an umbrella inside is a huge no-no. It's said to bring bad luck to you (and to the person next to you who just got poked in the eye!). Umbrellas date back to ancient China and ancient Egypt where they were used to shade emperors and pharaohs from the Sun. It wasn't until the 1600s that umbrellas were used as protection from wet weather in Europe. Back then, some people believed that objects used outside should never be used indoors. They may have thought opening an umbrella inside offended the home's guardian spirits, and, as a result, a storm of misfortune could rain down.

In And Out

In Greece, Ireland, and the United States, if someone comes into your house from one door, they should leave through the same door. If they exit through a different door, it's believed they'll take all the luck with them!

Adios!

Want to get rid of an annoying visitor but don't know how? Let a broom do your dirty work! In Latin America, leaving an upside-down broom standing behind the door will magically remind unwanted guests that they have something else to do, and they'll go!

HOW DID THAT START? BREAKING A MIRROR = SEVEN YEARS BAD LUCK

Be careful with that mirror! Breaking it supposedly brings seven years of bad luck. This well-known superstition may go back to ancient cultures that believed a person's reflection not only showed their physical appearance but was also a doorway to their soul, and so shattering a mirror was like damaging your soul. And what about the seven years? The ancient Romans believed a person's body renewed itself every seven years, so—good news!—luck would come back if you waited long enough. Hmmmm... were you hoping for a more logical explanation? Try this: Years ago, mirrors were extremely expensive and fragile, so this superstition may have been another way of saying "take care of our nice things!"

SWEEP TALKING!

There's a big pile of superstitions about sweeping!

Sweeping at night is bad luck. Why? Before electricity, sweeping in the dark, or the moonlight, meant you might sweep away a valuable item you didn't realize you'd dropped.

Always sweep out the back door, so your troubles are behind you.

When you move to a new house, buy a fresh broom and start off with a clean sweep!

Always store your broom bristle-end up for good luck.

In The Kitchen And At The Table

WHAT'S COOKIN'?

Jewish people believe that if you always keep something in your oven, your family will never be hungry. It doesn't have to be food—some people store baking pans in there.

On Your Feet

In Poland, don't sit down while a cake is baking in the oven or the cake will "sit down" too, meaning it won't rise.

Have A Knife Day

One old superstition says if you drop silverware on the floor, a visitor will arrive soon. So... who's coming over?
dropped knife = man
dropped fork = woman
dropped spoon = child
Drop all three and you'll have a party!

RHYME TIME
"Stir with a knife, stir up strife."

74

HOW DID THAT START?
DON'T SPILL THE SALT

In many cultures, spilling salt is said to bring mega bad luck. To reverse it, you must quickly throw a pinch of salt over your left shoulder with your right hand. Why so salty? Although the origins of this superstition are murky, salt has been a very valuable and rare resource throughout history, so the person who dared spill something so expensive suffered some serious side-eye. Since some people believed that your guardian angel hovered over your right shoulder and evil lurked over your left shoulder, the evil was to blame for your clumsy behavior. By tossing salt at it—not too much, though, because that wasted salt adds up!—you thwarted its power. Or could this superstition be another one of those warnings not to mess with the expensive stuff?

Another Salty Superstition

"Pass the salt, pass the sorrow" is an old saying that discourages handing the salt shaker directly to someone at the table or you'll be handing them bad luck. Instead, set it down on the table where they can pick it up.

DOWN NOT UP

It's unlucky to leave chopsticks standing up in a bowl of rice. Why? In China, chopsticks standing straight up resemble incense used to mourn the dead. In Japan, they resemble the Japanese number four, which represents death. Instead—and to show good manners—lay your chopsticks flat across your bowl.

Food

TORTILLA TELLS ALL

In Mexico, dropping a tortilla is believed to mean unwelcome company is coming, and burning a tortilla means someone's going to get married. If you're making tamales, be sure your temper doesn't flare—they won't fluff up right if you cook them while angry!

Feeling A Bit Stale

In the southern United States, it's said you should never eat both ends of a loaf of bread before you eat the middle or you won't be able to "make ends meet," which means you won't have enough money. The truth? It's best to eat the heels of the bread last, as they keep the squishy middle of a loaf from drying out.

BUTTER FINGERS

Pretend you're living back in Colonial America and—whoops!—you dropped a slice of buttered bread.
HOW DID IT LAND?
Butter side down = bad luck
(Well, duh—it's now too dirty to eat!)
Butter side up = expect a visitor soon

BES-TEAS!

When you pour tea in Iran, if any tea leaves float to the top of the glass, it's believed you will have guests. How many guests, you ask? Count the number of tea leaves to find out!

Spoiler Alert

Spilling milk is considered bad luck in most countries except Ireland. There, milk is said to be the favorite drink of fairies. Share this treat and they'll be extra kind to you!

Chew On This

According to Turkish legend, you should never chew gum at night or it will turn into the flesh of the dead.

SIP, SIP, HOORAY!

Superstition is brewing in the United Kingdom!

If you spill your tea, a stranger will soon visit.

If the tag falls off the teabag, you'll misplace something that week.

If the sugar stays undissolved at the bottom of your cup, someone has a crush on you.

RECIPE FOR A WISH

Before you eat a slice of cake or pie, cut off the point and save it for last. When you eat the point, you get to make a wish.

Wishbone

Making a wish on a wishbone is often the highlight of Thanksgiving dinner in the United States. But make no bones about it—you can do it any time of year.

HOW DID THAT START?

The wishbone origin story goes back to the Etruscans, an ancient civilization who lived in what is now Italy. They believed that chickens had the power to tell the future. They'd draw a circle on the ground and divide it into wedges—like the way you cut a pie—and write a letter of the alphabet inside each wedge. Grain was sprinkled in each wedge, and a rooster was placed in the middle. The local priests would ask the rooster an important question about the city's future and then watch to see which wedges the rooster ate from. They got their answer from those letters.

After the fortune-telling rooster died, its bones were left out to dry in the Sun. The V-shaped wishbone was used as a lucky charm, and anyone who walked by would stroke it while making a wish.

Enter the Romans. They borrowed the Etruscans' lucky wishbone idea, but they didn't have enough chickens to go around. So they began breaking the bone into two. More bones—and wishes—for everyone! Then the Romans introduced the wishbones to Europe. Germany used geese wishbones and often tried to predict the weather with them. In Britain, some people would balance the bone on their nose before making a wish and breaking it.

When the Pilgrims left Britain and sailed over to Plymouth Rock, there weren't many chickens, but wild turkeys were everywhere. "That'll work!" they thought and began making wishes on turkey bones. But the term "wishbone" didn't actually come into use until the mid-1800s. After Abraham Lincoln declared Thanksgiving a national holiday, the post-feast wish became a Turkey Day tradition.

A HELPING HAND FROM SCIENCE

If you really want your wish to come true, here are four ways—based on the science of physics—to increase your chances of getting the lucky break!

★ Choose the thicker side of the bone
★ Dry hands = a better grip
★ Grab the bone as close to the center of the V as you can
★ Don't twist the bone as you pull

HOW TO MAKE A WISH

1. Take the wishbone from a chicken or turkey—it's a V-shaped bone—and pull off all the meat and skin. Leave it out to dry for two or three days until it's brittle. Be patient. If it's not completely dry, it will bend instead of break.

2. Hold onto one end of the wishbone while someone else holds the other end. Both make a silent wish, then ready, set... pull until the wishbone breaks.

3. The one who gets the longer piece, or the "lucky break," will have their wish come true. If it's an even split, both your wishes will come true.

No Bones About It

Most birds have a furcula—that's the proper name for the wishbone—and scientists believe some dinosaurs had one, too! The furcula helps make a bird's skeleton strong enough for flight.

At School

Many kids write with a lucky pencil, wear lucky clothes, give their teacher a lucky greeting, or eat lucky foods in the hope that the right answers will land on the test page. But superstitions don't make us smarter, and they don't make us magically ace the math quiz. What they can do is give us a boost of self-confidence. While a positive outlook is always a plus, hitting the books is the best magic of all.

Do you have a unique ritual or lucky charm to help you ace a test?

To The Point
Some students believe that if you take a test with the same pencil you used to study with, the pencil will remember the answers. Others sharpen their pencil right before a test. Why? Sharp pencil = sharp mind.

A Cut Above
In Egypt—and really everywhere—be careful with scissors! It's considered bad luck to open and close scissors without cutting anything. It's also bad luck to leave them open.

LUCKY or UNLUCKY? It all depends...

LUCKY

Eating a KitKat
The candy is pronounced "kitto katto" in Japanese. This sounds like "*kitto katsu*," which means "win without fail."

Eating a spoonful of curd and sugar
In India, this combo is believed to pump up concentration and focus.

Wearing red underwear
In the Philippines and China, red is a lucky color.

Homophones (words that sound the same but have different meanings) play a big part in superstitions.

UNLUCKY

Eating seaweed soup
In South Korea, it's believed slippery foods make the info you learned slip right out of your brain.

Eating an egg
In Vietnam, foods shaped like zeros are best avoided.

Taking a bath or washing your hair
In India and South Korea, it's believed that if you do this, everything you've learned could go down the drain.

Walking About

HOW DID THAT START?
NEVER WALK UNDER A LADDER

Almost everywhere in the world, walking under a ladder is believed to bring bad luck. Sure, you could get thunked on the head by a falling paint can, but safety probably wasn't the reason this superstition came about. Some guess it goes back to an ancient belief that a triangle was a sacred shape, and a ladder propped against a wall forms a triangle. The ancient Egyptians would place a ladder inside tombs so that in the afterlife, the dead could climb up to the heavens. They believed the triangular space under the ladder was filled with spirits, and the spirits got cranky when disturbed by humans. Others have said a ladder's triangular shape represents the Christian belief in the Holy Trinity, and walking through or "breaking" the Trinity shows disrespect. Whether you believe in the superstition or not, our vote is safety first. Just walk around!

OK—so you didn't listen and walked under the ladder. Never fear! What's done can be undone. All you need to do is cross your fingers until you see a dog, or spit on your shoe. We know which one we'd rather do!

RECIPE FOR A WISH

If you see a postal worker or a red truck, cross your fingers and make a wish. Keep your fingers crossed until you see a dog, and the wish will come true.

After You

Pardon me, coming through! In the United Kingdom and France, passing another person on the stairs is thought to be bad luck. This superstition may go back to the narrow stone staircases in medieval castles—you didn't want to give your enemies the opportunity to turn around and stab you from behind. Yikes!

Step To It

In Sweden, stepping on a maintenance cover marked with a "K" is good luck, while stepping on a cover marked with an "A" is believed to be bad luck. In Norway, all maintenance covers have numbers, and stepping on one with the number 40 is said to bring bad luck. Someone must tap you three times on the back to instantly reverse the bad luck.

Brain Drain

In the United Kingdom, walking over three drain covers in a row is considered unlucky. Want to reverse the bad luck? Just walk over them backward.

Road Trip

GETTING READY TO GO

You're about to leave on a trip in Serbia or Iran when—SPLASH!—your friends and family spill water behind you. Since water flows, it's believed to make your trip go smoothly.

In Russia and Ukraine, sit on your suitcase and take a deep breath before a trip to guarantee a lucky journey.

In the northeastern United States, friends and family will sometimes throw coins on the floor of a new car for luck—and to scoop up to pay tolls. It's called "car coining."

Poop Power
Yucky bird poop on your car is a sign of good luck, so don't wash it off so fast!

Mess Up Your Ride
Some people believe you should scratch your new car yourself with a coin to ward off an accident or other damage.

Keeping It Wheel
In India, place lemons under the four tires of a new car then run them over. The squirting of sour citrus is thought to protect against future accidents or misfortunes.

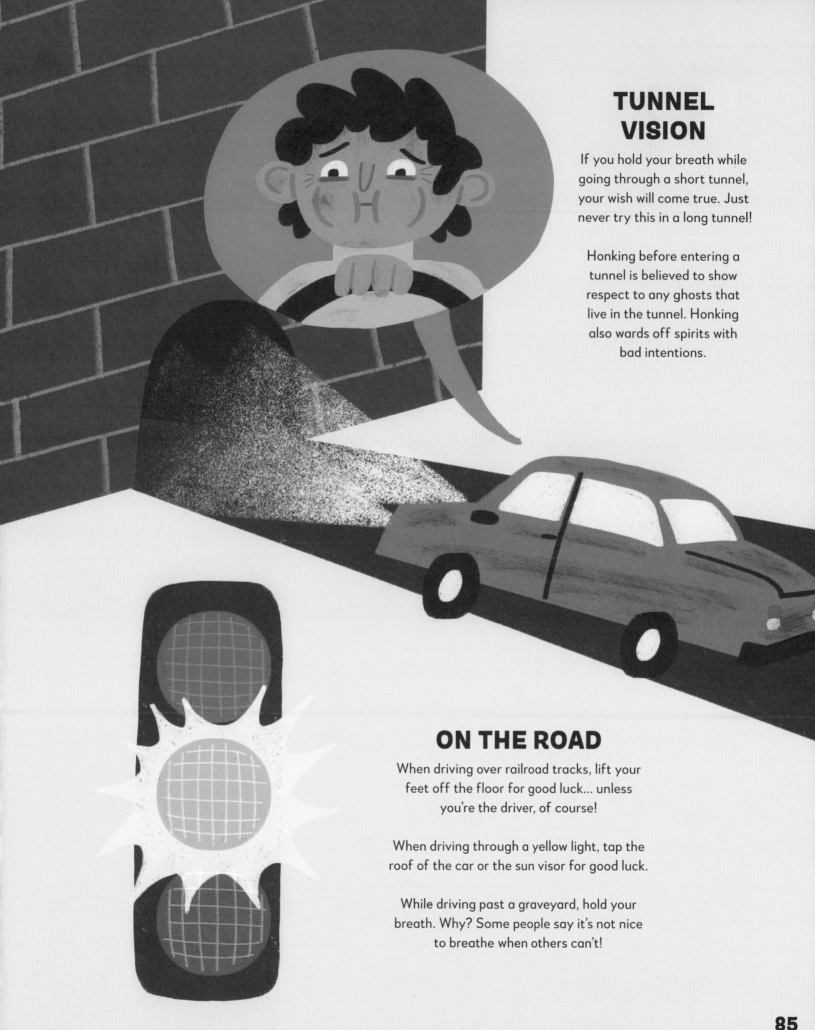

TUNNEL VISION

If you hold your breath while going through a short tunnel, your wish will come true. Just never try this in a long tunnel!

Honking before entering a tunnel is believed to show respect to any ghosts that live in the tunnel. Honking also wards off spirits with bad intentions.

ON THE ROAD

When driving over railroad tracks, lift your feet off the floor for good luck... unless you're the driver, of course!

When driving through a yellow light, tap the roof of the car or the sun visor for good luck.

While driving past a graveyard, hold your breath. Why? Some people say it's not nice to breathe when others can't!

On A Boat

SEAS THE DAY

Sailors used to get tattoos of a lucky rooster and a pig on their feet. Why a rooster and a pig? It's not like they're ace swimmers. On a boat, these animals were kept in wooden crates that floated, so the rooster and pig had a better chance of making it to shore if the boat went down. And if you could grab hold of their crate, you had a better chance, too!

We're Not Kitten! Don't Rock The Boat.

A cat onboard = good weather.
A cat overboard = a storm's coming.
If a black cat walks onto a boat then back off again = the boat's going to sink.

LUCKY or UNLUCKY?
It all depends...

LUCKY	UNLUCKY
✳ A pineapple onboard	✳ A bunny onboard
✳ A sailor wearing a gold hoop earring	✳ Changing the name of your boat
✳ Seeing an albatross or cormorant	✳ A black suitcase on a fishing boat

Dirty Dishes

Never ever wash a coffee mug in the US Navy, or it's believed you may cause a ship to end up on the ocean floor. Sailors and officers drink out of their same grimy, crusty mug day after day, year after year! Talk about flavored coffee!

Stormtrooper

Don't whistle on a boat, as you risk "whistling up a storm."

A Sinking Feeling

In China, if you flip over a whole cooked fish, it's believed a fisher's boat somewhere will capsize.

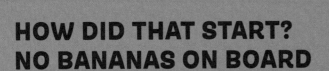

HOW DID THAT START?
NO BANANAS ON BOARD

Never bring bananas on a boat or misfortune will blow in. This superstition may go back hundreds of years to when boats from the Caribbean had to quickly deliver bananas to far off lands before the fruit spoiled. The crew couldn't slow down to fish, so they often went hungry. There's another theory that deadly spiders would hide in banana bunches, and another that—whoops!—banana peels caused slips and falls on deck.

On Stage

LUCKY or UNLUCKY?
It all depends...

LUCKY

✻ An elderly person purchases the first ticket for the first performance

✻ A cat backstage (except if it runs across the stage during a performance)

✻ Starting a performance 13 minutes late

✻ Shoes squeaking when an actor first appears on stage

UNLUCKY

✻ Whistling anywhere near the stage or clapping backstage

✻ Saying the last line of the play during a rehearsal or the night before a performance

✻ Giving an actor a bouquet of real flowers before a show

✻ Peacock feathers or a picture of an ostrich on stage

✻ A good dress rehearsal

TRIPPING UP

If an actor trips while making their first entrance, it's said they'll forget their lines. But if an actor falls down while on stage, the play will have good fortune.

HOW DID THAT START? THE SCOTTISH PLAY

Never, ever, EVER utter the word "Macbeth" anywhere in a theater or a dressing room. Legend has it that William Shakespeare's tragedy *Macbeth* is the unluckiest play of all, bringing extreme misfortune upon its actors. If you absolutely must chat about this play, only call it "the Scottish play" (because it takes place in Scotland).

So why is the M-word off-limits? It may be the play's three witches who chant lines such as "Double, double toil and trouble." Many people believed strongly in witchcraft when the play was first performed in the early 1600s, so actors and the audience probably worried that if certain names were said, it could unleash negative forces.

But what if you say the dreaded word? Luckily, there's a fix!
1. Exit the dressing room or theater immediately.
2. Spin counterclockwise three times.
3. Spit.
4. Recite either this line from *Hamlet*: "Angels and ministers of grace defend us!" or this line from *A Midsummer Night's Dream*: "If we shadows have offended, think but this and all is mended, that you have but slumbered here, whilst these visions did appear." Both *Hamlet* and *A Midsummer Night's Dream* are famous Shakespeare plays.
5. Knock on the dressing room or theater door and request permission to come back in.

NOT EASY BEING GREEN

Many actors believe wearing a green costume is unlucky, which is a big problem if you're cast as Peter Pan or Shrek! Back before electric lights, limelight was used to spotlight actors. It wasn't powered by the citrus fruit but instead by a chemical compound. Limelight's bright light had a hint of green and so, in the stage's greenish glow, actors dressed in green were almost invisible to the audience—and no actor ever wants that!

THE GHOST LIGHT

Boo! Actors are told to always leave a light on in an empty theater. If they don't, ghosts will cause mischief in the darkness. The reality? Backstage is often cluttered with furniture, props, and costumes, so in total darkness, someone could get hurt.

"Break A Leg!"

Never wish an actor or a musician "good luck" before a performance. Instead say "break a leg!" Why? No one knows for sure, but it could be because...

In ancient Greece, audiences stomped their feet instead of clapping their hands.

During Shakespeare's time, British actors would bow dramatically with a bent knee at curtain call, which was known as "breaking the leg."

In vaudeville theaters in the United States in the early 1900s, ensemble actors waiting offstage were warned not to "break," or cross, the "leg line" of the side curtains, because once they were officially onstage, the theater owner would have to pay them.

Many people believe that if they want something to happen, they have to wish for the opposite.

WHAT ABOUT OPERA SINGERS?

Instead of wishing an opera singer "good luck" before a performance, use the Italian phrase "*In bocca al lupo*" which means "In the mouth of the wolf." Again, you should never say "thank you," but "*crepi il lupo*" ("May the wolf die"). This phrase goes back to hunters wishing each other luck as they set off, but animal rights activists have been trying hard to change the response to "*viva il lupo*" ("long live the wolf"). We're here for that.

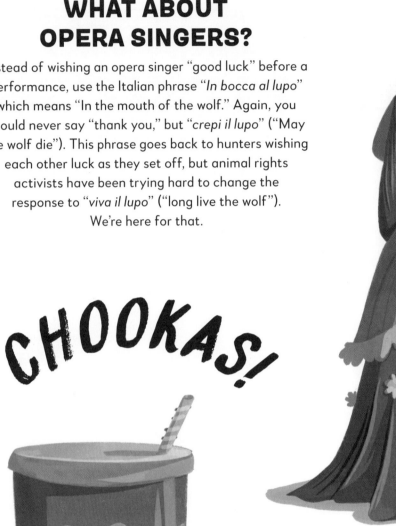

WINNER WINNER CHICKEN DINNER

Say "chookas!" to wish a performer good luck in Australia. This superstition supposedly goes back to the early 1900s, when actors would be treated to a chicken dinner whenever there was a sold out show. Before the show started, an actor would peek out at the audience. If the theater was full, they'd yell back to the cast, "Chook it is!" to let them know chicken would be served. This eventually morphed into "chookas!"

Superstitions Of Creative People

ARTISTS

Pablo Picasso would not throw away his fingernail clippings or hair trimmings for fear he'd lose part of his "essence."

Frida Kahlo included black cats in several of her paintings. Art lovers can't agree if the felines represent good luck or bad luck.

FASHION DESIGNERS AND MODELS

Yves Saint Laurent believed that if his bulldog sat on any outfit from a new collection, that outfit would become a bestseller.

Coco Chanel's lucky number was five. She named her famous perfume Chanel No. 5 and presented her clothing collections on May 5 (5/5) for good luck.

Christian Dior thought the number 13 was lucky and insisted there be exactly 13 models in his shows.

Jason Wu sews a feather into one garment in his fashion shows for good luck.

Heidi Klum keeps her own baby teeth in a little bag that she used to carry with her at all times for luck.

MUSICIANS AND COMPOSERS

The composer Pyotr Ilyich Tchaikovsky took a two-hour walk every day. The walk could not be a minute more or less, otherwise Tchaikovsky believed he'd have bad luck composing that day.

Beyoncé insists on an hour of alone time with her favorite playlists before performing.

John Philip Sousa wore a brand-new pair of white leather gloves to conduct every band concert to avoid bad luck. He conducted more than 15,550 concerts—that's a lot of gloves!

Before becoming a superstar, Ariana Grande ate a chocolate donut before every audition for luck.

AUTHORS

Dr. Seuss believed he'd get creative ideas if he wore a hat. He owned hundreds of different hats.

Charles Dickens carried a compass with him to be sure he slept facing north. He thought that was the best direction for creativity.

The poet Langston Hughes would only write letters in bright green ink.

NAILED IT!

Celebrated opera singer Luciano Pavarotti insisted on performing with a bent nail in his pocket as a good luck charm, but it had to be one he'd found backstage. In opera houses all around the world, stagehands would scatter a few along his path from the dressing room to the stage so the show could go on!

Sports And Famous Athletes

Athletes are known for being extremely superstitious. Even though they train intensely, many athletes get very nervous before a game, which isn't surprising, because unpredictable things can happen. Superstitious rituals often calm the butterflies and help athletes feel more in control until they're able to let their skills kick in.

BASEBALL

Pitcher Steve Kline refused to wash his baseball cap during the entire baseball season. He said the dirt kept him "grounded." The St. Louis Cardinals once held a "Steve Kline Hat Day" where fans got their own factory-made dirty hat.

Third baseman Wade Boggs was called "Chicken Man," because he had to eat chicken before every game.

Relief pitcher Turk Wendell chewed exactly four pieces of black licorice on the mound and always brushed his teeth in between innings. His lucky number was 99, and he insisted every amount of money in his contract ended in 99. His contract with the New York Mets was for $9,999,999.99!

LUCKY or UNLUCKY?
It all depends...

When it comes to baseball superstitions, the bases are loaded!

LUCKY

✳ Wearing a rally cap—a regular baseball hat worn backward, sideways, or inside out—if your team is down in the last inning
✳ Sticking a wad of gum on the bill of your cap
✳ Pointing skyward after a home run

UNLUCKY

✳ Stepping on the foul line
✳ Lending your bat to a teammate or changing bats after two strikes
✳ Talking about a no-hitter or perfect game before the game is over

BASKETBALL

Michael Jordan always wore his University of North Carolina basketball shorts under his Chicago Bulls uniform.

Kevin Garnett ate a peanut butter and jelly sandwich before every game.

LeBron James tosses a handful of chalk into the air before games.

ICE HOCKEY

Sidney Crosby of the Pittsburgh Penguins was voted the NHL's Most Superstitious Player! "Sid the Kid" never lets anyone touch his stick after he tapes it. If they do, he takes all the tape off and starts over.

Wayne Gretzky had a lot of pregame rituals. He would always fire his first warm-up shot to the right of the goal and drink a Diet Coke, a glass of ice water, a Gatorade, and another Diet Coke—in that order—before game time.

SOCCER

Cristiano Ronaldo makes sure his right foot steps onto the pitch first and insists on being the last player out the tunnel.

Before a corner, penalty, or free kick, Lionel Messi always puts the ball down with both hands and takes the same number of steps backward before kicking the ball.

THE LUCKY SHIRT

Brazilian superstar Pelé once gave away his lucky soccer shirt to a fan. Afterward, he fell into a scoring slump. Pelé desperately wanted his shirt back, but he had no clue how to find it, so he hired a private detective. The detective searched and searched and finally managed to track Pelé's shirt down. Delighted, the soccer star started scoring goals again. Years later, the detective told him the truth: He'd never found the lucky shirt but had given him one of his other match shirts instead!

FOOTBALL

Linebacker Brian Urlacher ate two chocolate chip cookies before every game.

Kicker Jake Elliott eats a slice of pizza and a slice of cheesecake the night before each game.

During his whole professional career, the quarterback Tom Brady wore the same shoulder pads that were first given to him during his freshman year at college.

Football Coaches Do It Too!

Coach Les Miles would pull up grass from the side of the field and eat it before every game, and coach John Madden refused to let his team leave the locker room until running back Mark van Eeghen had burped!

TENNIS

During changeovers in his matches, Rafael Nadal takes one sip from each of his two water bottles and places them back in the exact same position. He also makes sure both of his socks are at the exact same height.

Serena Williams always tied her shoelaces the exact same way, wore the same socks for an entire tournament, and bounced the ball five times before her first serve.

Naomi Osaka uses fancy footwork to avoid stepping on lines and logos on the court.

GOLF

Tiger Woods always wears a red shirt for the final round of a tournament and marks his ball with a 1932 quarter, because that was the year his dad was born, and his dad taught him how to putt.

Christina Kim believes she'll have bad luck if she steps on the edge where the fairway meets the green.

FANS PLAY THE SUPERSTITION GAME, TOO

Any diehard sports fan will tell you that when watching your team, it's important to wear your lucky game-day jersey, eat your lucky pregame meal, blast your lucky playlist, sit in your lucky spot, and hold or kiss your lucky memorabilia. What do you do?

Skiing

Alpine ski racer Lindsey Vonn wore everything in the same color on race day, from her ski pants to her underwear.

Surfing

Surfer Laird Hamilton was raised in Hawai'i, and he carried a Ti leaf with him. According to Polynesian superstition, the shiny leaf offers protection, and Laird felt it would always carry him home.

Rodeo

Rodeo star Chet Johnson never ate chicken before he rode because, as he said, "you are what you eat."

Snowboarding

Snowboarder Eva Adamczyková would draw a fake mustache on her upper lip for luck. Her fake mustache was still on her face when she stepped onto the podium in 2014 to receive her Olympic gold medal!

FRIEN
COLO
NUMB
AND OTHER
RANDOM STUFF

DSHIP, RS, ERS,

Do you tug your friend's ear on their birthday? Fear the number 13? Would you dare ride the waves on a yellow surfboard? Or hang upside down on top of a castle to kiss a magic stone? Do you wear red underwear on New Year's Eve? Or throw scoops of ice cream on the floor? It seems that somewhere in the world there's a superstition or tradition about pretty much anything and everything!

Friendship

RECIPES FOR A WISH

Do you have two friends with the same name? Stand in between them and make a wish!

If you and your friend say the same word at the exact same time, quickly lock your pinkie fingers together and each make a wish. Then, speak the other's name at the same time to make it come true.

If you open a nutshell and find two nuts inside, share the second one with a friend. Before you eat them, both of you can make a wish. Then, count to three, and whoever says "Lucky nut!" first will have their wish granted.

SWEET WORDS

In Azerbaijan, if you spill pepper, it means you'll soon have an argument with a friend. But if you quickly sprinkle sugar on the pepper, it'll sweeten things and prevent any quarrelling.

See You On The Other Side

Don't say your farewells to a friend while standing on a bridge, or it's believed you may never see each other again.

BFFs Stick Together

If you and your bestie are walking side by side and something in your path forces you to separate and each walk around a different side, you both need to say "bread and butter" three times, or else it's believed you'll stay apart forever.

PEPPERY PALS

Be careful when sharing a plate of nachos! Superstition says you should never directly hand your friend a hot pepper, or you'll get into a fiery argument. Instead, let them pick it up themselves.

Babies

SLOBBER

If you kiss a baby on the lips in Nigeria, legend says they'll spend their entire adult lives drooling!

Spell It Out

It's believed to be good luck if your initials spell a word.

Songs Take Root

Long ago in the United States, if a baby's first nail clippings were buried underneath a tree, it was believed the baby would grow up to have a beautiful singing voice.

WHEN I GROW UP

Proshtapulnik is a tradition in Bulgaria that celebrates a toddler starting to walk. A bunch of items that symbolize different jobs—such as a soccer ball, a toy police car, a paintbrush, and a chef's hat—are put on a low table. The toddler takes cute, wobbly steps to the table, and the first item they pick up is said to determine their future career! A similar pick-and-choose event called a *doljabi* is done on a baby's first birthday in South Korea.

That's Some Baby You Have There

In many cultures around the world, when you see a newborn, you should tell the parents, "Wow—your baby is so ugly!" Seriously. It's one of those superstitions that has us saying the opposite of what we mean, so if you call a baby "cute" or say something complimentary, it's believed you may attract negative energy to the kid. **Word of caution:** Only say this to parents who believe this superstition, otherwise it's next-level rude!

Money

"FIND A PENNY, PICK IT UP, ALL DAY LONG YOU'LL HAVE GOOD LUCK!"

Just check that the penny is heads side up before grabbing it, because many people believe that's the lucky side. If you find a penny tails side up, flip it over and leave it so whoever finds it next will have good luck.

Finders Keepers

After you pick up a coin in Poland, blow on it so the luck comes to you and not the person who dropped the coin.

Just Keep On Walking

In Nigeria and some Caribbean countries, don't pick up money from the ground. If you do, it's said you'll lose more money than you found— or even turn to stone!

ADDS UP

The idea that "money attracts money" is shared around the globe. It's believed if you always carry a coin in your pocket, wallet, or purse, money will find its way to you. And never give someone an empty wallet as a gift—always tuck some money inside first.

It's A Date

It's extremely lucky to find a coin minted the year you were born. And a coin from a leap year is extra lucky!

Money Talks

Have an itchy palm? To many people around the world, that means you're about to get some money!

RHYME TIME

"A purse on the floor, is money out the door." In Latin America and China, you should never leave your bag on the floor. It's believed if you disrespect your money, it will up and leave you!

HOW DID THAT START? MONEY TREE

Does money really grow on this tree? We wish! The Money Tree—scientific name *Pachira aquatica*—is said to bring good fortune to those who keep it in their home. One Chinese legend about the Money Tree is the story of a poor farmer who prayed for good fortune. Then, one day, he noticed a beautiful plant growing in his barren field. He cared for it and began to grow other plants from its seeds. He sold these to the villagers and became the wealthiest person in the village! Fast forward to the 1980s when a Taiwanese truck driver took several *Pachira aquatica* plants and braided their trunks together to create a single woven tree. Someone called it a Money Tree, connected it with the legend of the farmer, and a superstition was born. Suddenly, it became a popular gift!

Happy New Year

Out with the old, in with the new! Get up and start moving—you can't wait around for good luck in the coming year.

CLEAN UP (OR NOT) FOR A FRESH START

In Uruguay, throw buckets of water on the street and entrance to your house to clear away bad energy.

In Cuba, be sure to sweep out toward the street to get rid of all the past year's negativity.

In the United States, don't do laundry on New Year's Day, or you will wash away all your luck.

In the Philippines, throw open your windows and doors at midnight to let the old year escape.

In Ecuador, burning a newspaper-stuffed scarecrow on a big bonfire at midnight banishes the negativity of the old year.

In the Hillbrow neighborhood of Johannesburg, South Africa, people toss their unwanted furniture out of the window and onto the street to rid their life of clutter for the coming year. Watch out below!

THROW THINGS

In Greece and Turkey, hurl a pomegranate against your front door at midnight. The more seeds that fall out, the more luck you'll have.

In Switzerland, drop scoops of ice cream on the floor all night long for good fortune.

In Denmark, toss a plate at your friend or neighbor's house to wish them good luck. But it's much kinder and less dangerous to leave a pile of broken dishes at their front door instead. Save up chipped dishes throughout the year—don't break them just for this!

Move Forward

In Colombia, carry a suitcase around the block on New Year's Eve and you'll travel to great places in the coming year.

In Brazil, jump over seven ocean waves at midnight and make a wish on each wave.

Dress For Success

In Chile, Brazil, Mexico, and Peru, wear red or yellow underwear to attract love and wealth in the coming year. Some say you get more luck if you wear your colorful underwear backward!

PAPAS TELL THE FUTURE

In Peru, the pick-a-potato game predicts how much money you'll have in the coming year. Place three potatoes—one unpeeled, one half peeled, and one fully peeled—under your sofa or your bed. At exactly midnight, reach under without looking and grab the first potato you touch. Which potato did you get?
The half-peeled potato = it'll be a normal year.
The unpeeled potato = lots of money in the year ahead.
The peeled potato = you won't have a lot of money in the new year.

New Year's Eats

These New Year's eats are believed to serve up luck and fortune. Hope you're hungry!

In the southern United States, eat Hoppin' John (black-eyed peas mixed with rice and salt pork) collard greens, and cornbread. The veggie's green color symbolizes dollar bills, the round black-eyed peas symbolize coins, and the golden cornbread symbolizes, well... gold. The dish was introduced to the United States by enslaved people from West Africa.

In Pennsylvania and the Midwestern United States, gobble down a heaped plate of sauerkraut and pork. Pigs move forward to find food and in the new year, you also want to move forward, and the strands of sauerkraut symbolize long life.

In Norway and Sweden, dive into a bowl of sweet rice pudding sprinkled with cinnamon. Keep a look out for the one almond hidden in the pudding. If you scoop it up, you get the good luck. This sweet treat is also enjoyed on Christmas Eve.

In the Netherlands, eat *oliebollen* (donut-like dumplings dusted with powdered sugar) sold from street carts on New Year's Eve.

In Spain, Cuba, Central American, and South American countries, munch on 12 grapes. At midnight, pop them in your mouth one by one at each chime of the clock for twelve months of good luck. Make a wish on each grape. A sour grape means a sour month.

In Italy, eat *cotechino con lenticchie* (green lentils with sausages). The round lentils and the sausages sliced into disks look like coins and symbolize good luck and prosperity.

In Greece, help yourself to a slice of *Vasilopita* cake at midnight to celebrate the life of Saint Basil. There's a hidden coin baked inside. If you get the piece with the coin, you'll have good luck for the year.

In Poland, eat pickled herring at the stroke of midnight. The fish's silvery coloring represents wealth.

In Bulgaria, nibble on *banitza*. Baked into these cheese pastries are little pieces of paper with different fortunes written on them.

In Nigeria, feast on lentils and rice to bring prosperity. Rice swells when it cooks, symbolizing an abundance of happiness and luck.

In the Philippines, don't eat chicken on New Year's Eve. Chickens scratch backward for their food, so by eating chicken, you too will be destined to "scratch in the dirt" for food in the year ahead, meaning there won't be a lot to eat.

In Japan, slurp toshikoshi soba (buckwheat noodles) at midnight. Because of their shape, noodles symbolize long life, so the longer the better!

Happy Birthday!

PARTY CRASHERS

Hooray—you're another year older! Before turning up the tunes and hanging the balloons, you may want to peer into the shadows. Many early civilizations believed spirits would try to pay you a visit on your birthday, and that's probably how birthday parties began. People would gather around the birthday person on their big day and make lots of noise to scare any spirits away!

ALL EARS

Wish someone a happy birthday in Italy, Hungary, and Argentina by giving them a (gentle!) tug on their earlobe. Long ears were once a symbol of long life, so the goal was to pull your earlobes down to your ankles. Ouch!

Your Birthday Starts... NOW!

In Russia and Germany, never ever celebrate a birthday before the actual day or it's believed the birthday person and the overeager partygoers will experience a year of bad luck. Same goes for saying "happy birthday" or giving gifts.

You Butter Believe It

In eastern Canada, some kids get "greased" on their birthday. Friends and family try to sneak up on the birthday kid and smear butter on their nose to make them too slippery for bad luck to take hold.

HOW DID THAT START?
BLOWING OUT CANDLES ON A CAKE

While the ancient Greeks baked round cakes and lit candles on them to honor the moon goddess Artemis, it was the Germans in the 1700s who made flaming cakes a birthday party thing. On the morning of their birthday—called *Kinderfeste*—German kids were given a cake with the number of candles of their age plus one extra large candle called "the light of life" in the center. The candles were constantly relit all day, because the cake couldn't be eaten until after dinner. When it was cake time, if you blew out the big candle in one breath, it was believed you'd live to see another birthday. Life was hard then, and people died from the most random stuff, so you needed all the luck you could get! Over time, the single candle morphed into the superstition that the birthday person must make a silent, secret wish as they blow out all the candles. If all the candles go out in one breath, the wish will come true. If they can't huff and puff them all out—or if they reveal their wish—they're fresh out of luck. But the older you are, the more candles there are on your cake and the more lung power you need. So take a deep breath, Gramps!

Numbers

Do you have a lucky number? Around the world, many people share similar positive and negative feelings about certain numbers. Other numbers are considered lucky in one place and unlucky someplace else. Let's see how it all adds up!

UNLUCKY 13

One of the most common superstitions in North America and Europe is that the number 13 brings misfortune. The fear of 13 is so widespread it has its own word in the dictionary: triskaidekaphobia. People go to great lengths to avoid this number. Did you know that more than 80 per cent of high-rise buildings in the Western world don't have a 13th floor? They skip straight from 12 to 14. Many airplanes don't have a row 13, and lots of hospitals don't have a room 13.

So, what's so unlucky about 13? As with other superstitions that have evolved over time and across cultures, there are many theories about how this fear started and who's to blame.

Blame Loki

In Norse mythology, Baldur (the god of light and joy) threw a banquet for 12 gods and decided to leave trickster Loki off the invite list. Bad idea. Angry and jealous, Loki showed up anyway, increasing the guest count to 13. He tricked Baldur's brother into killing Baldur with a poisoned arrow, and this fatal act unleashed Ragnarok, which brought darkness and doom upon the world.

Blame The Last Supper

In Christianity, Judas Iscariot (one of Jesus' 12 apostles) was the 13th guest at the Last Supper. Judas went on to betray Jesus, which led to Jesus' crucifixion. Once again, 13 proved to be a deadly number.

Let's Talk About Friday the 13th...

Friday was once considered *almost* as unlucky as 13, so when you combine the two, some people come down with a bad case of friggatriskaidekaphobia, or the quaking fear of Friday the 13th. What's so wrong with Friday? It is the start of the weekend after all! But long ago, some people decided that it wasn't a good day. However, historians have looked back at major world events and determined that no more bad things happen on a Friday than any other day of the week!

13 IS LUCKY FOR SOME!

In Italy and India, 13 is a lucky number, and it's music superstar Taylor Swift's lucky number, too. She explained in an interview: "I was born on the 13th. I turned 13 on Friday the 13th. My first album went gold in 13 weeks. My first number one song had a 13-second intro. Every time I've won an award, I've been seated in either the 13th seat, the 13th row, the 13th section, or row M, which is the 13th letter. Basically, whenever a 13 comes up in my life, it's a good thing."

LUCKY BLACK CAT?

Eating with 13 people is never a cat-astrophe at The Savoy hotel in London, because Kaspar comes to the rescue! Kaspar is a lucky black cat carved out of wood. Whenever 13 people dine at the hotel, Kaspar is placed in a chair to be the 14th guest. With a napkin tied around his neck, he is served every course along with everyone else!

NUMBER 3

Three is a very powerful number that people believe can be good or bad luck. "Third time's the charm" or "bad luck comes in threes"—your choice!

NUMBER 4

Four is super unlucky in China, Japan, Vietnam, South Korea, and other East Asian countries. People avoid using four in addresses, phone numbers, and in the numbering of floors and rooms. If you give a gift of cups or sweets, you should always put three or five in a box—never four. The fear of the number four, known as tetraphobia, is because of homophones. In all these languages, the pronunciation of the number four sounds very similar to the word for "death." And 14 and 24 are extra unlucky—14 sounds like "will certainly die" and 24 sounds like "easy to die."

NUMBER 7

Seven is extremely lucky in most Western cultures, and many people claim it as their favorite number. So many things are grouped in sevens...
7 days of the week
7 colors in the rainbow
7 continents
7 wonders of the ancient world
7 notes on a musical scale
Can you think of others?

NUMBER 8

Eight is great! In China, eight is the luckiest number. Although not a perfect homophone, the word for eight in Chinese sounds like the word for "wealth." In Japan, the shape of the number symbolizes growth and good fortune. It was no accident that the opening ceremony of the Beijing Olympics in 2008 started at 8:08pm on 8/8/08!

NUMBER 9

Nine is an excellent number in Chinese culture because it sounds like the word "everlasting." In Thailand, since the number three—or any multiple of three—is lucky, nine is triple lucky, especially because the word "nine" sounds similar to the word for "progress."

NUMBER 11

When the clock strikes 11:11, make a wish. It's the only time that all the numbers are the same. And go for an extra special wish on November 11 (11/11) at 11:11!

NUMBER 17

Seventeen is the ultimate unlucky number in Italy. Italians write 17 using the Roman numerals XVII. These numbers can be rearranged to form the Latin word "VIXI," which translates to "I have lived," but actually means "my life is over." And no one wants that! Alitalia (Italy's former national airline) didn't have a row 17 on their planes, and many buildings don't have a 17th floor.

At the 2006 winter Olympics in Turin, Italy, the 17th curve on the bobsled track was called "Senza Nome," which means "without name."

Colors

RED

Red is a very **lucky** color in many East Asian countries. Eating red beans in Vietnam and giving money in red envelopes in China are both believed to bring good fortune.

However, red is **unlucky** in Korea. Never sign a living person's name in red ink—it's as if you're wishing they weren't alive.

YELLOW

Yellow is a **lucky** color in Chile. Many students there dress in yellow clothing for exams.

Some surfers in South Africa and Australia won't use an **unlucky** yellow surfboard. They believe that "yum yum yellow" attracts sharks. But scientists now know that sharks are actually colorblind, so this superstition is a wipe out.

BLUE

Actors in the United States and the United Kingdom used to be told that wearing the **unlucky** color blue onstage would cause them to forget their lines. The truth? Blue dye was expensive, and theater owners didn't want to spend a lot of money on blue costumes!

When a bride gets married, an old British rhyme instructs her to wear "something old, something new, something borrowed, something blue." **Lucky** blue was supposed to bring everlasting love.

GREEN

In Ireland, green is the **lucky** color of shamrocks and the color worn by leprechauns.

Sailors once believed that having anything green on a boat was **unlucky**. After all, green is the color of land.

PURPLE

In Costa Rica, the **lucky** purple Santa Lucia flower is given as a gift on the New Year's holiday to attract money. Many Costa Ricans will keep a dried flower in their wallet all year long.

It was once considered **unlucky** to wrap gifts in purple paper or wear purple to the opera in Italy, because purple was for funerals. It's also a color of mourning in Brazil.

ORANGE

In India, the orange-colored spice saffron is considered to be very **lucky**.

We couldn't find any **unlucky** superstitions about the color orange. Maybe you know one?

COLOR ME LUCKY

In Thailand, there's a lucky color for each day of the week. Some older Thai people still wear the color connected to that day.

Monday → Yellow
Tuesday → Pink
Wednesday → Green (daytime) or Gray (night)
Thursday → Orange
Friday → Light Blue
Saturday → Purple
Sunday → Red

Superstitious Places Around The World

BLARNEY STONE (BLARNEY, REPUBLIC OF IRELAND)

KISS THE STONE FOR THE GIFT OF THE GAB

Journey to Blarney Castle to plant a smooch on the famous Blarney Stone, but don't expect it to be easy! The stone is set into the castle's high wall, so you must climb to the top of the castle and then hang backward and upside down from the parapet while holding onto railings. It's believed that once your lips touch the stone, you'll become a smooth talker and be able to convince anyone of anything.

Lincoln's Lucky Nose (Springfield, Illinois, USA)
RUB A PRESIDENT'S NOSE FOR GOOD LUCK

A massive bronze bust of Abraham Lincoln—the United States' 16th president—sits in front of his tomb at the Oak Ridge Cemetery. If you visit, rub Abe's shiny nose for good luck. So many people have touched his nose that holes have worn through, and metalsmiths have had to repair them. No one "nose" how the superstition began, but people often like to rub the noses and feet of statues for luck.

Einstein's Intelligent Nose (Washington, D.C., USA)
RUB A GENIUS' NOSE FOR A SPARK OF SMARTS

Speaking of noses, why not pay a visit the huge bronze Albert Einstein statue on the grounds of the National Academy of Sciences before your next exam? If you rub the nose, it's believed the famous physicist's genius will rub off on you. Albert's nose shines bright from all the wishes!

Trevi Fountain (Rome, Italy)
TOSS A COIN FOR A RETURN TRIP TO ROME

This magnificent 18th century marble fountain is probably the most famous fountain in the world. Close your eyes and use your right hand to fling a coin over your left shoulder. It's believed if it lands in the fountain, you'll return to Rome. The city cleans out the fountain weekly, and more than $1 million in coins is collected each year. This money is then donated to local charities.

Fountain of Wealth (Suntec City, Singapore)
TAKE A WALK FOR GOOD LUCK

This enormous fountain in the middle of a shopping mall is said to overflow with positive "*qi*" energy. If you walk around the entire fountain three times with your right hand on the water the whole time, it's believed you'll be granted good luck. But you'd better lace up those sneakers though—it's a loooooong walk!

THE MOUTH OF TRUTH (ROME, ITALY)
RISK YOUR HAND IN THE ULTIMATE LIE DETECTOR

Bocca della Verità—the Mouth of Truth—is an enormous marble mask of a bearded man's face placed on an outside wall of the medieval Cosmedin church. He might look friendly, but beware! This mask can supposedly sniff out liars! As you place your hand inside the open mouth, have someone ask you a question. If you answer with the truth, you can pull your hand out no problem. But if you lie, it's believed the mouth will bite your hand off!

LAUGHING BUDDHA (HANGZHOU, CHINA)
RUB A BIG BELLY FOR GOOD LUCK

In the ancient Lingyin Temple, there's an enormous stone statue of the Laughing Buddha, or Budhai. If you rub its massive, round belly, it's believed you will receive good fortune, health, and wealth. According to legend, the Laughing Buddha's jolly laughter gets rid of all suffering.

Magic Owl of Dijon (Dijon, France)
TOUCH AN OWL TO MAKE YOUR WISH COME TRUE

For more than 300 years, a small stone owl carved into a corner of Dijon's oldest church has been the city's unofficial mascot. Touch the bird with your left hand while placing your right hand on your heart and make a wish, and it's believed it will come true. Owls have long been symbols of wisdom.

Hagia Sophia (Istanbul, Turkey)
TWIST YOUR THUMB AND YOUR SICKNESS WILL GO AWAY

Built in the 6th century as a place of worship, Hagia Sophia is a beautiful Byzantine domed building decorated with majestic mosaics and 140 stone columns. The building was first a cathedral, then a mosque, then a museum, then a mosque again. Stick your thumb into a small hole in the famous "Weeping Column." If you're able to turn your thumb in a complete circle and it comes out wet, it's believed your sickness will be cured. Not sick? Make a wish instead.

Lucky Tree Stump at the Apollo Theater (New York City, New York, USA)
RUB A TREE STUMP FOR A STANDING OVATION

During the late 1920s, unemployed talent used to perform around an elm tree in front of the Lafayette Theater hoping they'd get noticed by the management. If they were hired, they said it was because the tree gave them good luck. When the tree was cut down in 1934, the host of the Apollo Theater's Amateur Night rescued the stump and placed it on a pedestal in the wings of the theater. Over the years, stars including Ella Fitzgerald, The Jackson 5, and H.E.R. have rubbed it for luck before stepping onto the stage.

Shoe Trees (Lyndonville, New York, USA)
FLYING SNEAKERS FOR A SOLE-FUL WISH

In upstate New York, send your wishes soaring. Tie your laces together then toss your sneakers—old ones that you're ready to get rid of!—into one of the town's several Shoe Trees. If your shoes catch on a branch, it's believed your wish will come true.

WISHING TREES (TAI PO, HONG KONG)
TOSS ORANGES TO MAKE WISHES COME TRUE

The magical banyan trees of Lam Tsuen in Hong Kong are famous for making wishes come true, especially during the Lunar New Year. Originally, you'd write your wish on a piece of paper, tie it to a mandarin orange, and toss the fruit up into the tree's branches. If the orange got caught, it was believed your wish would come true. If your orange plummeted to the ground, it was said your wish was too greedy. For the health of the Wishing Trees, wishes are now written on slips of multicolored paper and tucked into plastic oranges or tossed onto bamboo racks.

The Thirteen Club

You are cordially invited to
become an honorary member of

THE THIRTEEN CLUB

where we meet superstitions face-to-face
and challenge them one by one. This club
is not for the faint of heart. Are you
brave enough to join us?

The Thirteen Club was a real thing back in the 1800s. A group of 13 men gathered in New York—and later in London and other cities—with one goal: to prove that superstitions were false. The original Thirteen Club was founded by Captain William Fowler who had always found 13 to be a lucky number. But it took him a full year to recruit the other 12 members because so many people were too scared to take part. Women also created their own club, too.

On Friday, January 13, 1882 at 8:13 pm, the Thirteen Club met at a hotel for the first time. All 13 members had to walk under a ladder to enter Room 13. They sat together at a table lit by 13 candles and decorated with spilled salt and mirrors to break. They ate 13 courses of superstitious foods and opened umbrellas inside.

AND DO YOU KNOW WHAT HAPPENED?
No one got sick. No one lost all their money. Everyone was perfectly fine. And the club continued to meet once a month for years to come.

As the world has changed, a lot of old superstitions, beliefs, and traditions have been tossed aside. Yet many continue to hang around. The great thing is that YOU have the power to decide what you believe and what you don't, what you let scare you and what you don't, what wishes you send out into the universe, and—most of all—what kind of luck you bring to yourself and the people around you. The ultimate good luck charm is **YOU!**

"A black cat crossing your path signifies that the animal is going somewhere."
Groucho Marx, actor and comedian

Index